Title :

Easy Anti-Inflammatory Recipes Cookbook

Sub-Title :

60 Healthy Delicious Meals with High-Quality Photos

By Shirley Macy

Introduction

Inflammation is a silent intruder, often creeping into our lives without warning, bringing with it discomfort and a host of health issues. But what if you could combat it deliciously? Welcome to "Easy Anti-Inflammatory Recipes Cookbook" by Shirley Macy, your new ally in the fight against inflammation. This cookbook is more than just a collection of recipes; it's a gateway to a healthier lifestyle, offering a simple yet effective approach to eating well and feeling better.

Imagine savoring meals that not only tantalize your taste buds but also nourish your body from the inside out. Shirley Macy, a renowned nutritionist and culinary expert, has meticulously curated 60 recipes that are mouth-watering and designed to reduce inflammation. Each recipe is accompanied by stunning, high-quality photographs that will inspire you to get cooking. This cookbook has everything from hearty breakfasts to satisfying dinners and even indulgent yet healthy desserts.

But this cookbook is about more than just back great recipes. It's a journey towards a healthier you. Each dish is crafted with ingredients known for their anti-inflammatory properties, ensuring that every bite contributes to your well-being. The best part? These recipes are easy to follow, making healthy eating accessible to everyone, regardless of their cooking skills. Whether you're a seasoned chef or a beginner in the kitchen, "Easy Anti-Inflammatory Recipes Cookbook" will guide you through each step with clarity and ease.

Don't wait to embrace a healthier lifestyle. "Easy Anti-Inflammatory Recipes Cookbook" is available in both Kindle and Paperback formats, ensuring access to these life-changing recipes in whatever format suits you best. Start your journey towards a healthier, happier you by grabbing your copy today. With Shirley Macy's expert guidance and delicious recipes, you're just a few pages away from transforming your diet and combating inflammation the tasty way!

Copyright

what is inflammation ?

Acute Inflammation: This starts rapidly and quickly becomes severe. Signs and symptoms are usually only present for a few days but may persist for a few weeks. Examples of diseases, conditions, and situations that can result in acute Inflammation include acute bronchitis, an infected ingrown toenail, a sore throat from a cold or flu, a physical trauma or injury, and dermatitis.

Chronic Inflammation: refers to long-term Inflammation that lasts several months or even years. It can result from a failure to eliminate whatever was causing acute Inflammation, an autoimmune response to a self-antigen (the body attacks its cells), a chronic irritant of low intensity that persists, or other factors. Diseases and conditions associated with chronic Inflammation include asthma, chronic peptic ulcer, tuberculosis, rheumatoid arthritis, chronic periodontitis, ulcerative colitis and Crohn's disease, chronic sinusitis, and chronic active hepatitis.

Common symptoms of Inflammation include redness, swelling, pain, and heat in the affected area. These are caused by increased blood flow and an accumulation of white blood cells in the tissue. Chronic Inflammation can eventually cause several diseases and conditions, including some cancers, rheumatoid arthritis, atherosclerosis, periodontitis, and hay fever.

anti inflammatory guideline

Guidelines for managing inflammation generally involve a combination of dietary choices, lifestyle changes, and, if necessary, medication. Here are some general recommendations:

1. Dietary Changes:

Increase Omega-3 Fatty Acids: These are found in foods like fish (especially salmon and mackerel), flaxseeds, and walnuts. Omega-3s are known to reduce inflammation. Eat More Fruits and Vegetables: They are high in antioxidants and phytochemicals that can reduce inflammation.

Choose Whole Grains: Whole grains contain more fiber, which can help reduce inflammation. Cut Back on Refined Sugars and Carbs: High sugar intake and refined carbohydrates can increase inflammation in the body.

Spices: Some spices, like turmeric and ginger, have anti-inflammatory properties.

2. Lifestyle Changes:

Regular Exercise: Moderate exercise can help reduce inflammation.

Adequate Sleep: Poor sleep can increase inflammation, so aim for 7-9 hours of quality sleep per night.

Stress Management: Chronic stress can trigger inflammation, so meditation, yoga, or even simple breathing exercises can be beneficial.

3. Medication:

Over-the-Counter Options: Non-steroidal anti-inflammatory drugs (NSAIDs) like ibuprofen and naproxen can be effective.

Prescription Medications: Doctors may prescribe stronger anti-inflammatory medications for chronic inflammatory conditions.

4. Avoid Inflammatory Foods:

Trans Fats: Found in fried foods, fast food, and commercially baked goods.

Excessive Alcohol: Moderate consumption is critical.

Processed Meats: These can contribute to inflammation.

5. Stay Hydrated:

Drinking enough water is essential for reducing inflammation and overall health.

6. Consult with Healthcare Professionals:

It's essential to consult with healthcare professionals before making significant changes to your diet or lifestyle or before taking a new medication.

Remember, these guidelines are general and might not apply to everyone. Individual needs can vary, especially if there are specific health conditions involved.

how to preuent and control inflammatory

Preventing and controlling inflammation involves a combination of lifestyle changes, dietary adjustments, and possibly medical interventions, depending on the cause and severity of the rash. Here are some general guidelines:

1. Healthy Diet:

○ Consume a diet rich in fruits, vegetables, whole grains, and lean protein. These foods are high in natural antioxidants and polyphenols—plant protective compounds.

○ Include anti-inflammatory foods like tomatoes, olive oil, green leafy vegetables (spinach, kale, and collards), nuts like almonds and walnuts, fatty fish (salmon, mackerel, tuna, and sardines), and fruits such as strawberries, blueberries, cherries, and oranges.

2. Avoid Inflammatory Foods:

○ Reduce intake of foods that can promote inflammation, such as fried foods, sugary beverages, refined carbohydrates, lard, processed meats, and margarine.

3. Regular Physical Activity:

○ Engage in regular physical activity. Moderate exercise is beneficial for controlling inflammation. This can include walking, swimming, cycling, or yoga.

4. Maintain a Healthy Weight:

○ Excess weight can lead to increased inflammation in the body. Losing weight can reduce this inflammatory response.

5. Manage Stress:

○ Chronic stress contributes to inflammation. Techniques like mindfulness, meditation, deep breathing, and yoga can help manage stress.

6. Adequate Sleep:

○ Ensure you get enough sleep. Poor sleep can exacerbate inflammation.

7. Avoid Smoking and Limit Alcohol Consumption:

○ Smoking is a significant risk factor for chronic inflammation, and excessive alcohol consumption can also contribute to inflammation.

8. Regular Medical Check-Ups:

○ Regular check-ups with your healthcare provider can help monitor and manage any conditions contributing to chronic inflammation.

9. Medications and Supplements:

○ In some cases, medications or supplements might be recommended. These can include anti-inflammatory drugs (like NSAIDs), fish oil supplements, or curcumin (a compound in turmeric). However, always consult a healthcare provider before starting any new medication or supplement.

Remember, it's essential to consult with a healthcare professional for personalized advice, especially if you have a chronic condition or are experiencing severe or persistent inflammation.

TABLE OF CONTENTS

Chapter Name 03: Dinners Recipes

Chapter Name 04: Midnight Snack Recipes

Chapter Name 05: Salads Recipes

Chapter Name 06: Soup Recipes

Chapter 01 : Breakfasts Recipes

Recipe 01: Avocado and Spinach Green Smoothie

Servings For: (02)

Prepping Time: 10 min

Cooking Time: 0 minutes

Difficulty: Easy

Indulge in the goodness of a refreshing and healthy Avocado and Spinach Green Smoothie, perfect for kick-starting your day with a burst of nutrients. This anti-inflammatory breakfast smoothie is a delightful blend of fresh avocados, spinach, and other wholesome ingredients, offering a balanced start to your morning.

Preparation Steps

- Combine avocado, spinach, banana, Greek yogurt, honey, and almond milk in a blender.
- Blend on high speed until smooth and creamy. Add ice cubes for a chilled smoothie.
- Taste and adjust sweetness if necessary.
- Pour into glasses and serve immediately.

Ingredients

- One ripe avocado, peeled and pitted
- 2 cups fresh spinach
- One banana, sliced
- 1/2 cup Greek yogurt
- One tablespoon of honey or agave syrup
- 1/2 cup almond milk or water
- Ice cubes (optional)

Nutritional Facts: (Per serving)

- Calories: 150
- Protein: 12g
- Carbohydrates: 3g
- Fat: 10g
- Fiber: 1g
- Cholesterol: 180mg

Embrace a healthier lifestyle with this Avocado and Spinach Green Smoothie. Not only does it help in reducing inflammation, but it also offers a quick and delicious way to incorporate more greens into your diet. Perfect for busy mornings, this smoothie is a powerhouse of nutrition and taste!

Recipe 02: Sweet Potato Cubes Rocket Salad Wit Avocado and Pouched Eggs

Servings For: (02)

Prepping Time: 15 min

Cooking Time: 10 minutes

Difficulty: Easy

Delight your taste buds and boost your health with this anti-inflammatory breakfast recipe featuring sweet potato cubes, rocket salad, avocado, and poached eggs. This dish combines vibrant flavors and nutritious ingredients, offering a perfect start to your day.

Preparation Steps

- Preheat your oven to 200°C (400°F). Toss sweet potato cubes with olive oil, salt, and pepper. Spread on a baking sheet and roast for 15-20 minutes until tender.
- While roasting sweet potatoes, bring a pot of water to a simmer for poaching eggs.
- In a large bowl, combine rocket salad and lemon juice. Add roasted sweet potatoes and sliced avocado.
- Poach eggs in simmering water for about 3-4 minutes.
- Place poached eggs on top of the salad. Drizzle with balsamic vinegar if desired.

Ingredients

- Two medium sweet potatoes peeled and cubed
- 2 cups rocket salad (arugula)
- One ripe avocado, sliced
- Four eggs for poaching
- One tablespoon of olive oil
- Salt and pepper, to taste
- One teaspoon of lemon juice
- Two tablespoons of balsamic vinegar (optional)

Nutritional Facts: (Per serving)

- Calories: 350
- Protein: 12g
- Carbohydrates: 45g
- Fat: 16g
- Fiber: 9g
- Sugar: 7g

Start your day with this nutritious and delicious sweet potato cubes rocket salad. It's not just a meal; it's a vibrant, healthful experience that aligns perfectly with an anti-inflammatory diet. Enjoy the symphony of flavors and textures in every bite and feel energized for the day ahead.

Recipe 03: Quinoa With Nuts Milk and Berries

Servings For: (02)

Prepping Time: 10 min

Cooking Time: 20 minutes

Difficulty: Easy

This Instant Pot Egg and Spinach Frittata is a perfect recipe for those seeking a healthy, weight-loss-friendly breakfast. Packed with protein and greens, it's both nutritious and delicious, making mornings brighter and more beneficial.

Preparation Steps

- Rinse quinoa under cold water. Drain.
- In a saucepan, combine quinoa and almond milk. Bring to a boil.
- Reduce heat, cover, and simmer for 15 minutes or until quinoa is soft.
- Stir in cinnamon, salt, and half of the nuts.
- Serve in bowls, topped with berries, remaining nuts, and a drizzle of honey or maple syrup.

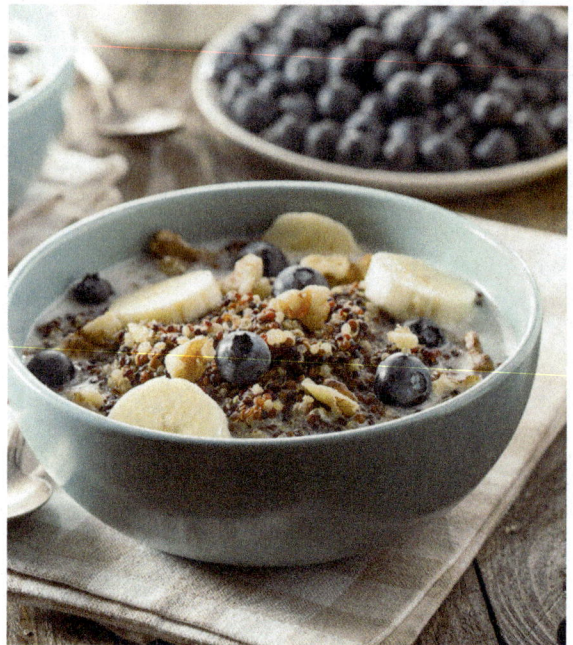

Ingredients

- 1 cup quinoa
- 2 cups almond milk
- 1/2 cup mixed berries (blueberries, strawberries, raspberries)
- 1/4 cup mixed nuts (almonds, walnuts, cashews), chopped
- 2 tbsp honey or maple syrup
- 1 tsp cinnamon
- A pinch of salt

Nutritional Facts: (Per serving)

- Calories: 320
- Protein: 10g
- Fiber: 6g
- Fat: 10g (healthy fats from nuts)
- Sugar: 8g (natural sugars)

Embrace a morning ritual that's satisfying and beneficial for your health with this Quinoa with Nuts, Milk, and Berries breakfast. Not only does it fuel your day, but it also supports your well-being with its anti-inflammatory properties. Enjoy a bowl and start your day with a smile!

Recipe 04: Chia Seed Pudding With Fresh Berries and Fig Slices

Servings For: (02)

Prepping Time: 15 minutes

Cooking Time: 0 minutes

Difficulty: Easy

Indulge in the perfect start to your day with this anti-inflammatory chia seed pudding, bursting with the goodness of fresh berries and fig slices. This delightful recipe tantalizes your taste buds and offers numerous health benefits, making it an ideal breakfast choice for those seeking a nutritious and delicious meal.

Preparation Steps

- Mix chia seeds with almond milk, honey, and vanilla extract in a bowl. Stir well.
- Let the mixture sit for 5 minutes, then stir again to break any clumps.
- Cover the bowl and refrigerate overnight, allowing the chia seeds to swell and absorb the liquid.
- In the morning, give the pudding a good stir. If it's too thick, add a little more milk.
- Serve in bowls or glasses, topped with fresh berries, fig slices, and a sprinkle of cinnamon.

Ingredients

- 1/4 cup chia seeds
- 1 cup almond milk (or any milk of choice)
- One tablespoon of honey or maple syrup
- 1/2 teaspoon vanilla extract
- 1/4 cup fresh berries (blueberries, strawberries, raspberries)
- Two fresh figs, sliced
- A pinch of cinnamon (optional)

Nutritional Facts: (Per serving)

- Calories: 210
- Protein: 6g
- Fiber: 9g
- Sugar: 12g (natural sugars from fruits)
- Healthy Fats: 8g

Wrap up your morning on a high note with this chia seed pudding. Not only is it a breeze to prepare, but it also packs a punch of essential nutrients. The combination of chia seeds, fresh berries, and figs provides a balanced blend of anti-inflammatory benefits, fiber, and natural sweetness, making it a wholesome choice for a busy morning or a leisurely weekend breakfast.

Recipe 05: Pancakes With Raspberries

Servings For: (04)

Prepping Time: 15 minutes

Cooking Time: 10 minutes

Difficulty: Easy

Indulge in a delightful breakfast with our "Pancakes with Raspberries" recipe. This dish not only tantalizes your taste buds but also offers anti-inflammatory benefits, making it a perfect start to your day. Enjoy the blend of fluffy pancakes and fresh, tangy raspberries in every bite.

Preparation Steps

- Mix flour, sugar, baking powder, baking soda, and salt in a large bowl.
- In another bowl, whisk together buttermilk, egg, and melted butter.
- Pour the wet ingredients into the dry ingredients and stir until just combined.
- Heat a non-stick pan over medium heat and lightly grease it.
- Pour 1/4 cup of batter for each pancake until bubbles form on the surface, then flip and cook until golden brown.
- Serve the pancakes with fresh raspberries and a drizzle of honey or maple syrup.

Ingredients

- 1 cup all-purpose flour
- Two tablespoons sugar
- One teaspoon of baking powder
- 1/2 teaspoon baking soda
- 1/4 teaspoon salt
- 1 cup buttermilk
- One egg
- Two tablespoons melted butter
- 1 cup fresh raspberries
- Honey or maple syrup for serving

Nutritional Facts: (Per serving)

- Calories: 280
- Protein: 6g
- Carbohydrates: 42g
- Fat: 10g
- Fiber: 3g
- Sugar: 12g

Our "Pancakes with Raspberries" recipe is more than just a breakfast; it's a wholesome experience. Each serving brings a perfect balance of sweetness and nutrition. This recipe is ideal for those seeking a healthy yet delicious start to their day. Enjoy the anti-inflammatory benefits and the irresistible taste of raspberries in this simple, satisfying meal.

Recipe 06: Banana and Almond Butter Toasts

Servings For: (02)

Prepping Time: 10 minutes

Cooking Time: 5 minutes

Difficulty: Easy

This simple yet delicious Banana and Almond Butter Toast recipe is a perfect anti-inflammatory breakfast option. Packed with the goodness of bananas and nutrient-rich almond butter, it's a healthy and satisfying start to your day.

Preparation Steps

- Two slices of whole-grain bread
- One ripe banana, sliced
- Two tablespoons of almond butter
- A pinch of cinnamon
- Honey (optional)

Ingredients

- One large eggplant, diced
- One can of chickpeas, drained and rinsed
- 2 cups tomato sauce
- One onion, finely chopped
- Two cloves garlic, minced
- 1 tsp cumin
- 1 tsp paprika
- Salt and pepper to taste
- 2 tbsp olive oil
- Fresh parsley for garnish

Nutritional Facts: (Per serving)

- Calories: 280
- Protein: 8g
- Fat: 15g
- Carbohydrates: 30g
- Dietary Fiber: 5g
- Sugar: 10g

This Banana and Almond Butter Toast offers a delightful taste and benefits your health with its anti-inflammatory properties. It's a quick and easy recipe, ideal for busy mornings or when you need a nutritious snack. Enjoy this wholesome treat, and start your day off right!

Recipe 07: Vegetarian Egg Muffins With Mushroom, Green Kale and Feta Cheese

Servings For: (06)

Prepping Time: 15 minutes

Cooking Time: 20 minutes

Difficulty: Easy

Indulge in a delightful and nutritious start to your day with these vegetarian egg muffins. Packed with the goodness of mushrooms, green kale, and feta cheese, these muffins are delicious and serve as a perfect anti-inflammatory breakfast option. Easy to prepare and packed with flavor, they're ideal for busy mornings or a leisurely weekend brunch.

Preparation Steps

- Preheat your oven to 350°F (175°C) and grease a muffin tin with cooking spray or olive oil.
- Whisk together eggs, milk (if using), salt, and pepper in a mixing bowl.
- Stir in the chopped kale, diced mushrooms, crumbled feta cheese, and red bell pepper.
- Pour the mixture into the prepared muffin tin, filling each cup about 3/4 full.
- Bake in the oven for 20 minutes or until the muffins are set and lightly golden.
- Allow to cool for a few minutes before serving.

Ingredients

- Six large eggs
- 1 cup chopped green kale
- 1/2 cup diced mushrooms
- 1/2 cup crumbled feta cheese
- 1/4 cup diced red bell pepper
- 1/4 cup milk (optional)
- Salt and pepper to taste
- Cooking spray or olive oil for greasing

Nutritional Facts: (Per serving)

- Calories: 120
- Protein: 9g
- Fat: 8g
- Carbohydrates: 4g
- Fiber: 1g
- Sugar: 2g

Enjoy these delightful vegetarian egg muffins as a healthy and satisfying breakfast. Their anti-inflammatory properties, thanks to ingredients like kale and mushrooms, make them a smart choice for a well-balanced diet. Perfect for meal prepping, these muffins can be stored in the refrigerator for a quick and easy breakfast throughout the week.

Recipe 08: Fresh Oatmeal Porridge With Apples, Honey, Nuts and Cinnamon

Servings For:
(02)

Prepping Time:
10 minutes

Cooking Time:
15 minutes

Difficulty:
Easy

Discover the delightful and healthful experience of making fresh oatmeal porridge with apples, honey, nuts, and cinnamon. This anti-inflammatory breakfast recipe tantalizes your taste buds and offers a nutritious start to your day. It's a perfect balance of sweet and savory, packed with flavors that comfort and energize.

Preparation Steps

- In a medium saucepan, bring water or milk to a boil. Add oats and salt, stirring occasionally.
- Reduce heat and simmer for 5 minutes.
- Add diced apple and cinnamon. Cook for another 5-10 minutes until the oats are soft and creamy.
- Remove from heat. Stir in honey and nuts.
- If desired, serve hot, garnishing with extra apple slices and a sprinkle of cinnamon

Ingredients

- 1 cup rolled oats
- 2 cups water or milk
- One apple, peeled and diced
- Two tablespoons honey
- 1/4 cup chopped nuts (almonds, walnuts, or pecans)
- 1/2 teaspoon ground cinnamon
- Pinch of salt

Nutritional Facts: (Per serving)

- Calories: 300
- Protein: 8g
- Carbohydrates: 55g
- Dietary Fiber: 6g
- Sugars: 20g
- Fat: 8g
- Sodium: 50mg

As you savor each spoonful of this warm, comforting oatmeal porridge, you'll enjoy a delicious breakfast and a healthier lifestyle. This easy-to-make, anti-inflammatory recipe is perfect for busy mornings or leisurely weekends, bringing a wholesome and satisfying start to your day.

Recipe 09: Yogurt Parfait With Assorted Berries and Nuts

Servings For: (02)

Prepping Time: 10 minutes

Cooking Time: 0 minutes

Difficulty: Easy

Discover the perfect start to your day with this yogurt parfait, combining the creamy goodness of yogurt with a colorful array of assorted berries and crunchy nuts. This delightful dish is delicious and packed with anti-inflammatory benefits, making it an ideal choice for a health-conscious breakfast.

Preparation Steps

- In a bowl, mix the Greek yogurt with vanilla extract and honey.
- In serving glasses, layer half of the yogurt mixture.
- Add a layer of mixed berries over the yogurt.
- Sprinkle a layer of chopped nuts.
- Repeat the layers with the remaining yogurt, berries, and nuts.
- Garnish with a sprinkle of cinnamon, if desired.
- Serve immediately or refrigerate until ready to eat.

Ingredients

- 1 cup plain Greek yogurt
- 1/2 cup mixed berries (blueberries, strawberries, raspberries)
- 1/4 cup mixed nuts (almonds, walnuts, pecans), chopped
- Two tablespoons honey
- One teaspoon of vanilla extract
- A pinch of cinnamon (optional)

Nutritional Facts: (Per serving)

- Calories: 280
- Protein: 12g
- Carbohydrates: 32g
- Fat: 12g
- Fiber: 4g
- Sugar: 20g
- Sodium: 45mg

Wrap up your morning routine with this simple yet exquisite yogurt parfait. It's a delightful mix of creamy yogurt, fresh berries, and crunchy nuts, all layered together to create a symphony of flavors and textures. Not only does it tantalize your taste buds, but its anti-inflammatory properties also provide a nutritious boost to kick start your day.

Recipe 10 : Broccoli and Feta Cheese Omelette With Rye Bread Toasts

Servings For: (2)

Prepping Time: 10 minutes

Cooking Time: 15 minutes

Difficulty: Easy

Embark on a culinary journey with this delightful Broccoli and Feta Cheese Omelette, complemented by crispy Rye Bread Toasts. This anti-inflammatory breakfast recipe tantalizes your taste buds and offers a wholesome start to your day. It's packed with nutritious ingredients, ensuring a balance of flavor and health.

Preparation Steps

- Steam the broccoli until tender and set aside.
- Whisk the eggs, garlic powder, salt, and pepper in a bowl.
- Heat olive oil in a pan, pour the egg mixture and cook for 2 minutes.
- Add the steamed broccoli and feta cheese over half of the omelet.
- Gently fold the omelet in half and cook until the eggs are set.
- Toast the rye bread slices to your preference.
- Serve the omelet hot with the toasted rye bread and garnish with fresh herbs.

Ingredients

- 1 cup chopped broccoli
- Four large eggs
- 1/2 cup crumbled feta cheese
- Two slices of rye bread
- Two tablespoons of olive oil
- Salt and pepper, to taste
- 1/4 teaspoon garlic powder
- Fresh herbs (such as parsley or chives) for garnish

Nutritional Facts: (Per serving)

- Calories: 350
- Protein: 20g
- Carbohydrates: 18g
- Dietary Fiber: 4g
- Sugars: 3g
- Fat: 22g
- Saturated Fat: 6g
- Cholesterol: 370mg
- Sodium: 540mg

Concluding this culinary experience, the Broccoli and Feta Cheese Omelette with Rye Bread Toasts stands as a testament to a meal that is as nutritious as it is delicious. Perfect for those seeking a healthy, anti-inflammatory breakfast, this dish is a beautiful blend of flavors and textures that promises to start your day on a high note.

Recipe 11: Chicken Fajitas With Vegetables

Servings For: (4)

Prepping Time: 20 minutes

Cooking Time: 15 minutes

Difficulty: Easy

Embark on a culinary journey with our Chicken Fajitas with Vegetables, a tantalizing anti-inflammatory lunch recipe. This dish delights your taste buds and offers health benefits, making it a perfect choice for a nutritious meal.

Preparation Steps

- Combine chicken slices with cumin, paprika, salt, and pepper in a large bowl.
- Heat olive oil in a skillet over medium heat. Add garlic and onion, sautéing until translucent.
- Add chicken to the skillet and cook until browned.
- Add bell peppers and cook for an additional 5 minutes.
- Warm tortillas in a separate pan.
- Assemble fajitas by placing chicken and vegetables in tortillas and garnish with cilantro.

Ingredients

- Two chicken breasts, thinly sliced
- One red bell pepper, sliced
- One green bell pepper, sliced
- One yellow bell pepper, sliced
- One onion, thinly sliced
- Two cloves garlic, minced
- Two tablespoons of olive oil
- One teaspoon of ground cumin
- One teaspoon of smoked paprika
- Salt and pepper to taste
- Four whole wheat tortillas
- Fresh cilantro for garnish

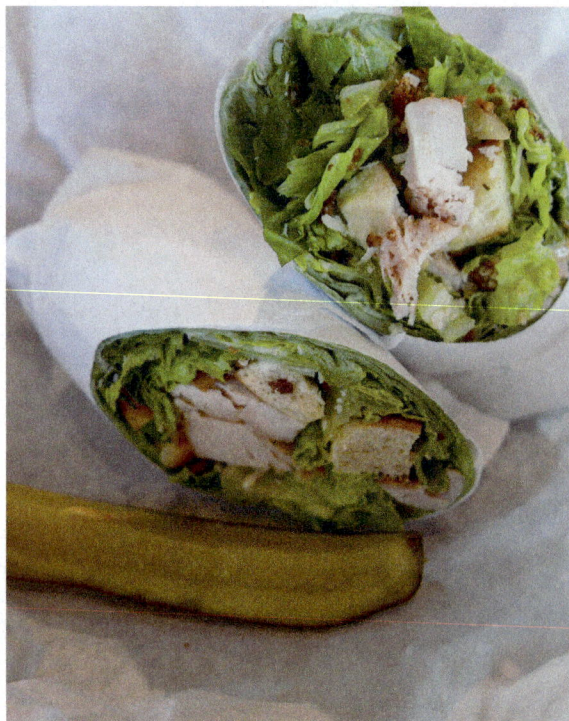

Nutritional Facts: (Per serving)

- Calories: 350
- Protein: 28g
- Carbohydrates: 33g
- Fat: 12g
- Dietary Fiber: 5g
- Sodium: 320mg

Conclude your meal with this vibrant Chicken Fajitas with Vegetables, a dish that brings flavor and health benefits to your table. It's a simple yet satisfying way to enjoy a wholesome meal that supports your well-being.

Recipe 12: Quinoa Tabouleh

Servings For: (04)

Prepping Time: 20 minutes

Cooking Time: 15 minutes

Difficulty: Easy

Quinoa tabouleh is a refreshing and healthy lunch option for those seeking anti-inflammatory benefits. This recipe combines the nutty flavor of quinoa with fresh herbs and vegetables, making it a delightful and nutritious choice for any day.

Preparation Steps

- Rinse quinoa under cold water. In a medium saucepan, bring 2 cups of water to a boil. Add quinoa and simmer for 15 minutes or until water is absorbed.
- Let the quinoa cool, then fluff with a fork.
- Combine cooled quinoa, cucumber, tomatoes, parsley, and mint in a large bowl.
- Whisk together olive oil, lemon juice, salt, and pepper in a small bowl.
- Pour the dressing over the quinoa mixture and toss well.
- Refrigerate for at least 1 hour before serving to enhance flavors.

Ingredients

- 1 cup quinoa
- 2 cups water
- One cucumber, diced
- Two medium tomatoes, diced
- 1/2 cup fresh parsley, finely chopped
- 1/4 cup fresh mint, finely chopped
- Three tablespoons olive oil
- Two tablespoons of lemon juice
- Salt and pepper, to taste

Nutritional Facts: (Per serving)

- Calories: 210
- Protein: 6g
- Carbohydrates: 33g
- Fat: 7g
- Dietary Fiber: 5g
- Sugar: 3g

Quinoa tabouleh is not just a tasty meal; it's a powerhouse of nutrition and health benefits. It's perfect for those looking to reduce inflammation and enjoy a light yet satisfying lunch. Easy to make and packed with flavor, it will become a favorite in your recipe collection.

Recipe 13: Thai Curry With Butternut Squash, Chickpeas, and Cilantro

Servings For: (04)

Prepping Time: 20 minutes

Cooking Time: 40 minutes

Difficulty: Medium

This Thai curry with butternut squash, chickpeas, and cilantro is a delightful and healthy lunch option. Rich in flavors and packed with anti-inflammatory benefits, it's a perfect choice for a nutritious meal.

Preparation Steps

- In a large pan, heat olive oil over medium heat. Add onions, garlic, and ginger, sautéing until fragrant.
- Stir in the red curry paste and cook for a minute.
- Add butternut squash and chickpeas, stirring to coat with the curry mixture.
- Pour in coconut milk and bring to a simmer. Reduce heat, cover, and cook until the squash is tender.
- Season with salt and pepper. Stir in half the cilantro.
- Serve hot, garnished with remaining cilantro.

Ingredients

- One medium butternut squash, peeled and cubed
- One can of chickpeas, drained and rinsed
- One can of coconut milk
- 2 tbsp Thai red curry paste
- One onion, finely chopped
- Two cloves garlic, minced
- 1 inch ginger, grated
- One bunch of cilantro, chopped
- 2 tbsp olive oil
- Salt and pepper to taste

Nutritional Facts: (Per serving)

- Calories: 350
- Protein: 8g
- Carbohydrates: 45g
- Fat: 18g
- Dietary Fiber: 9g
- Sugars: 5g

This Thai curry is a perfect blend of taste and health, ideal for an anti-inflammatory diet. The combination of butternut squash and chickpeas offers a satisfying meal that is both vegan and gluten-free, making it a versatile option for various dietary preferences.

Recipe 14: Baked Salmon Fillet With Broccoli and Vegetables Mix

Servings For: (04)

Prepping Time: 15 minutes

Cooking Time: 30 minutes

Difficulty: Medium

This delightful recipe for Baked Salmon Fillet with Broccoli and Vegetable Mix offers a perfect blend of nutrition and flavor. Rich in Omega-3 and packed with anti-inflammatory properties, it's an ideal choice for a healthy lunch.

Preparation Steps

- Preheat your oven to 375°F (190°C).
- Arrange the salmon fillets and vegetables on a baking sheet.
- Drizzle olive oil over the salmon and veggies.
- Season with garlic powder, thyme, salt, and pepper.
- Bake for 25-30 minutes until salmon is cooked and vegetables are tender.
- Serve warm with lemon wedges on the side.

Ingredients

- Four salmon fillets (6 ounces each)
- One large head of broccoli, cut into florets
- One red bell pepper, thinly sliced
- One yellow bell pepper, thinly sliced
- Two tablespoons of olive oil
- One teaspoon of garlic powder
- One teaspoon of dried thyme
- Salt and pepper, to taste
- Lemon wedges for serving

Nutritional Facts: (Per serving)

- Calories: 350
- Protein: 34g
- Carbohydrates: 15g
- Fat: 18g
- Omega-3 Fatty Acids: 2g
- Dietary Fiber: 4g

Wrap up your meal with this nutritious and satisfying dish that not only delights the taste buds but also boosts your health. The combination of tender salmon, crispy broccoli, and colorful bell peppers makes this meal a visually appealing and anti-inflammatory powerhouse. Perfect for a wholesome lunch, it's a dish that promises health and flavor in every bite.

Recipe 15: Turmeric Chicken Curry Rice Casserole

Servings For: (04)

Prepping Time: 20 minutes

Cooking Time: 45 minutes

Difficulty: Moderate

Discover the flavors of an anti-inflammatory lunch with this Turmeric Chicken Curry Rice Casserole. A delightful blend of spices, this dish is a treat for the palate and beneficial for your health.

Preparation Steps

- Preheat your oven to 375°F (190°C).
- In a skillet, sauté onions and garlic until translucent.
- Add the chicken, turmeric, cumin, and coriander. Cook until the chicken is browned.
- Mix in the cooked rice, coconut milk, and peas. Season with salt and pepper.
- Transfer the mixture to a casserole dish and bake for 30 minutes.

Ingredients

- 2 cups of cooked rice
- 1 lb chicken breast, cubed
- One tablespoon of turmeric powder
- One teaspoon cumin
- One teaspoon coriander
- One can of coconut milk
- One diced onion
- Two cloves garlic, minced
- 1 cup frozen peas
- Salt and pepper to taste

Nutritional Facts: (Per serving)

- Calories: 350
- Protein: 25g
- Carbohydrates: 40g
- Fat: 10g
- Fiber: 3g
- Sugar: 2g

Conclude your meal with a sense of accomplishment, knowing you've nourished your body with a delicious, anti-inflammatory dish. This Turmeric Chicken Curry Rice Casserole is perfect for a wholesome lunch, offering a balance of flavors and health benefits. Enjoy the comfort of a hearty meal while taking care of your well-being.

Recipe 16: Zoodles Spiralized Zucchini Noodles With Meatballs and Parmesan

Servings For: (04)

Prepping Time: 20 minutes

Cooking Time: 30 minutes

Difficulty: Medium

Indulge in a flavorful and healthy journey with this Instant Pot recipe for Salmon with Asparagus and Tomatoes with Herbs. Perfect for weight loss lunches, this dish blends succulent salmon with fresh vegetables and aromatic herbs, offering a delightful taste and nutritional benefits.

Preparation Steps

- Mix ground meat, breadcrumbs, egg, garlic, parmesan, salt, and pepper in a bowl. Form into meatballs.
- Heat olive oil in a pan and cook meatballs until browned and cooked.
- In a separate pan, sauté spiralized zucchini in olive oil for 3-4 minutes.
- Warm marinara sauce in a saucepan.
- Serve zoodles topped with meatballs, marinara sauce, and a sprinkle of parmesan. Garnish with basil.

Ingredients

- Four medium zucchinis, spiralized
- 1 lb ground turkey or beef
- 1/2 cup breadcrumbs
- 1/4 cup grated parmesan, plus extra for garnish
- Two cloves garlic, minced
- One egg
- 2 cups marinara sauce
- 1 tsp olive oil
- Salt and pepper to taste
- Fresh basil for garnish

Nutritional Facts: (Per serving)

- Calories: 350
- Protein: 26g
- Carbohydrates: 18g
- Fat: 18g
- Fiber: 4g
- Sugar: 6g
- Sodium: 480mg

Wrap up your meal with this delightful zoodles and meatballs recipe, a perfect combination of taste and health. Not only does it satisfy your pasta cravings, but it also supports your wellness journey with its anti-inflammatory benefits. Enjoy this mouth-watering lunch that's as nutritious as it is delicious!

Recipe 17: Brussel Sprouts With Red Peppers, Pancetta and a Balsamic Glaze

Servings For: (04)

Prepping Time: 15 minutes

Cooking Time: 20 minutes

Difficulty: Easy

Discover the delightful flavors of "Brussel Sprouts with Red Peppers, Pancetta, and a Balsamic Glaze," a perfect anti-inflammatory lunch recipe. This dish combines the nutty taste of Brussels sprouts with the sweetness of red peppers and the savory richness of pancetta; all brought together with a tangy balsamic glaze. Easy to prepare and packed with health benefits, it's an ideal choice for a nutritious and delicious meal.

Preparation Steps

- Preheat your oven to 400°F (200°C).
- Toss the Brussels sprouts and red peppers with olive oil, salt, and pepper on a baking sheet.
- Roast for 15 minutes until slightly tender.
- In a pan, cook the pancetta over medium heat until crispy.
- Add the roasted vegetables to the pancetta and stir.
- Drizzle with balsamic vinegar and cook for another 5 minutes.
- Serve warm and enjoy!

Ingredients

- 1 pound of Brussels sprouts, halved
- One red pepper, sliced
- 4 ounces of pancetta, chopped
- Two tablespoons of olive oil
- Three tablespoons of balsamic vinegar
- Salt and pepper to taste

Nutritional Facts: (Per serving)

- Calories: 250
- Protein: 8g
- Carbohydrates: 18g
- Fat: 17g
- Dietary Fiber: 5g
- Sugar: 5g

Savor this exquisite dish's rich and complex flavors, ideal for a refreshing and health-boosting lunch. Not only does it satisfy your taste buds, but it also provides essential nutrients beneficial for reducing inflammation. Whether you're seeking a quick lunch option or a new recipe to add to your repertoire, this dish is a delightful choice that promises to impress.

Recipe 18: Quinoa and Roasted and Fresh Vegetables

Servings For: (04)

Prepping Time: 15 minutes

Cooking Time: 30 minutes

Difficulty: Easy

Quinoa with roasted and fresh vegetables is a vibrant and healthy dish perfect for an anti-inflammatory lunch. The combination of fluffy quinoa and various colorful vegetables offers a nutritious and delicious meal that's easy to prepare.

Preparation Steps

- Preheat the oven to 400°F (200°C).
- In a medium saucepan, bring water to a boil. Add quinoa, reduce heat, cover, and simmer for 15-20 minutes until water is absorbed.
- Toss the red and yellow bell peppers, zucchini, and red onion with olive oil, garlic powder, salt, and pepper.
- Spread the vegetables on a baking sheet and roast for 20 minutes, stirring halfway through.
- Once the quinoa and vegetables are cooked, combine them in a large bowl.
- Stir in the fresh cherry tomatoes and garnish with fresh parsley.

Ingredients

- 1 cup quinoa, rinsed
- 2 cups water
- One red bell pepper, chopped
- One yellow bell pepper, chopped
- One zucchini, sliced
- 1 cup cherry tomatoes, halved
- One red onion, sliced
- Two tablespoons of olive oil
- One teaspoon of garlic powder
- Salt and pepper, to taste
- Fresh parsley for garnish

Nutritional Facts: (Per serving)

- Calories: 250
- Protein: 8g
- Fiber: 5g
- Fat: 7g
- Carbohydrates: 40g

This quinoa and roasted fresh vegetable dish is a feast for the eyes and a boon for your health. Its anti-inflammatory properties and high nutrient content make it ideal for a wholesome lunch. Easy to make and packed with flavor, it's a recipe that will become a staple in your healthy eating routine.

Recipe 19: Grilled Salmon With Stir-Fried Broccoli and Cauliflower

Servings For: (04)

Prepping Time: 20 minutes

Cooking Time: 30 minutes

Difficulty: Intermediate

Experience the perfect blend of flavors and health benefits with "Grilled Salmon with Stir-Fried Broccoli and Cauliflower." This anti-inflammatory lunch recipe tantalizes your taste buds and offers a nutritious boost. Ideal for those seeking a wholesome yet delicious meal, it combines the rich, savory taste of grilled salmon with the fresh, crunchy texture of stir-fried veggies.

Preparation Steps

- Preheat your grill to medium-high heat.
- Season the salmon fillets with salt, pepper, garlic powder, and paprika.
- Grill the salmon for about 5 minutes on each side or until cooked to your liking.
- Meanwhile, heat olive oil in a pan over medium heat and stir-fry the broccoli and cauliflower until tender-crisp.
- Serve the grilled salmon with the stir-fried broccoli and cauliflower. Garnish with fresh lemon slices.

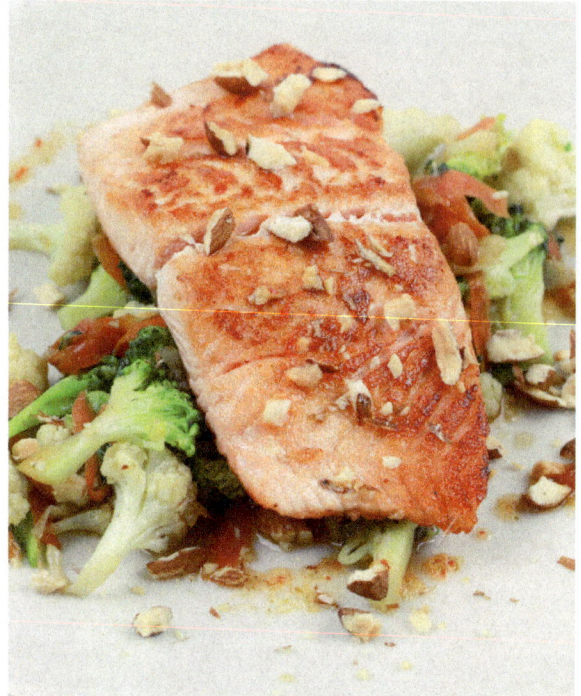

Ingredients

- Four salmon fillets
- One head of broccoli, cut into florets
- One head of cauliflower, cut into florets
- Two tablespoons of olive oil
- One teaspoon of garlic powder
- One teaspoon paprika
- Salt and pepper, to taste
- Fresh lemon slices for garnish

Nutritional Facts: (Per serving)

- Calories: 350
- Protein: 25g
- Carbohydrates: 10g
- Fat: 20g
- Fiber: 4g
- Sugar: 3g

Conclude your meal with a sense of satisfaction, knowing you've nourished your body with a meal that's as beneficial as delicious. This "Grilled Salmon with Stir-Fried Broccoli and Cauliflower" is more than just a lunch; it's a celebration of healthy eating that doesn't compromise flavor. Perfect for those on an anti-inflammatory diet or anyone looking for a tasty, health-conscious meal.

Recipe 20: Turkey Sandwich

Servings For:
(02)

Prepping Time:
15 minutes

Cooking Time:
5 minutes

Difficulty:
Easy

Embark on a journey to create a delightful, health-conscious turkey sandwich perfect for an anti-inflammatory lunch. This simple yet delicious recipe is designed to please your taste buds while contributing to your well-being.

Preparation Steps

- Toast the bread slices to your desired crispness.
- Spread Dijon mustard evenly on one side of each bread slice.
- Layer the turkey, avocado, tomato, onion, and lettuce on two bread slices.
- Drizzle olive oil and sprinkle salt and pepper on the fillings.
- Top with the remaining bread slices, mustard side down.
- Cut the sandwiches in half and serve immediately.

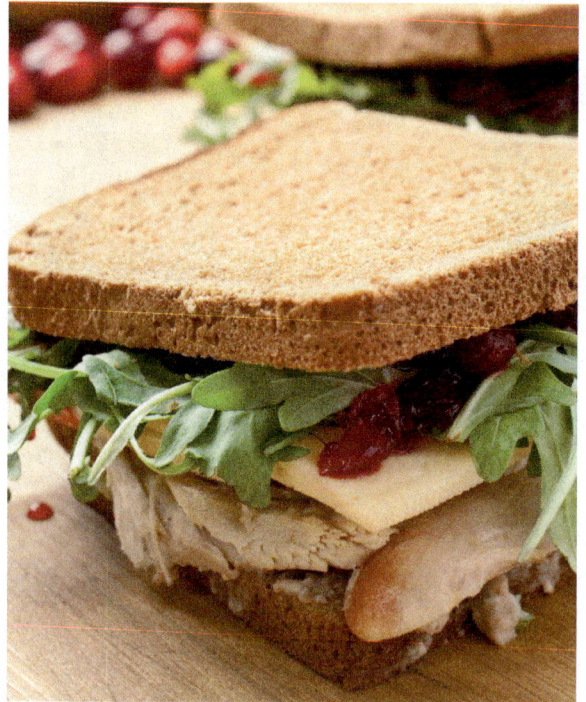

Ingredients

- Four slices of whole-grain bread
- 6 ounces of sliced turkey breast
- One avocado, sliced
- One tomato, sliced
- 1/2 red onion, thinly sliced
- Two lettuce leaves
- Two teaspoons of Dijon mustard
- One tablespoon of olive oil
- Pinch of salt and black pepper

Nutritional Facts: (Per serving)

- Calories: 350
- Protein: 25g
- Carbohydrates: 27g
- Fat: 17g
- Fiber: 6g
- Sodium: 540mg

Conclude your meal with a sense of satisfaction, knowing you've nourished your body with a turkey sandwich that's not only delicious but also tailored for anti-inflammatory benefits. This easy-to-make lunch is perfect for busy days, providing comfort and health in every bite.

Chapter 03 : Dinners Recipes

Recipe 21: Grilled Chicken Meat and Organic Veggies and Greens

Servings For: (04)

Prepping Time: 20 minutes

Cooking Time: 30 minutes

Difficulty: Moderate

Grilled chicken meat paired with a medley of organic vegetables and greens makes for a delightful anti-inflammatory dinner. This dish combines the richness of protein-packed chicken with the freshness of assorted veggies, creating a balanced and nutritious meal that's as pleasing to the palate as beneficial for health.

Preparation Steps

- Preheat the grill to medium-high heat.
- Season chicken breasts with garlic powder, paprika, salt, and pepper.
- Lightly coat vegetables with olive oil.
- Grill the chicken for 6-7 minutes per side or until fully cooked.
- Grill vegetables alongside the chicken, turning occasionally until tender and slightly charred.
- Serve grilled chicken with grilled vegetables and a handful of mixed greens.

Ingredients

- Four boneless, skinless chicken breasts
- One zucchini, sliced
- One red bell pepper, cut into strips
- 1 cup of broccoli florets
- 1 cup of mixed greens (spinach, kale, arugula)
- Two tablespoons of olive oil
- One teaspoon of garlic powder
- One teaspoon paprika
- Salt and pepper to taste

Nutritional Facts: (Per serving)

- Calories: 250
- Protein: 28g
- Carbohydrates: 8g
- Fat: 11g
- Fiber: 3g
- Sodium: 210mg

This grilled chicken with organic veggies and greens is not just a meal; it's a celebration of health and flavor. Rich in proteins and loaded with antioxidants, this dish is perfect for those looking to enjoy a hearty, anti-inflammatory meal that doesn't compromise on taste or nutrition. Enjoy this delightful dinner and feel the goodness with every bite.

Recipe 22: Pasta Stuffed With Ricotta and Spinach With Tomato Sauce

Servings For: (4)

Prepping Time: 20 minutes

Cooking Time: 35 minutes

Difficulty: Medium

Embark on a culinary journey with this delectable Pasta Stuffed with Ricotta and Spinach, smothered in a rich tomato sauce. This recipe, part of our Anti-Inflammatory Dinners series, is a treat for your taste buds and a boon for your health. Packed with the goodness of spinach, ricotta, and a tangy tomato sauce, it's a perfect blend of nutrition and flavor.

Preparation Steps

- Preheat your oven to 375°F (190°C).
- Mix ricotta, spinach, Parmesan, garlic, salt, and pepper in a bowl.
- Lay out pasta sheets and spoon the filling onto each. Roll them up and place them in a baking dish.
- Pour tomato sauce over the pasta rolls.
- Bake for 25-30 minutes until golden and bubbly.

Ingredients

- One pack of fresh pasta sheets
- 2 cups ricotta cheese
- 1 cup fresh spinach, chopped
- 2 cups tomato sauce
- 1/2 cup grated Parmesan cheese
- Two cloves garlic, minced
- 1 tsp olive oil
- Salt and pepper to taste

Nutritional Facts: (Per serving)

- Calories: 350
- Protein: 18g
- Carbohydrates: 35g
- Dietary Fiber: 4g
- Sugars: 4g
- Fat: 16g
- Saturated Fat: 8g
- Cholesterol: 30mg
- Sodium: 480mg

As you savor each bite of this Pasta Stuffed with Ricotta and Spinach, let the flavors transport you to a world of wholesome goodness. Not only does this meal satisfy your palate, but it also contributes to your wellness, aligning with the principles of Anti-Inflammatory Dinners. Enjoy this heartwarming meal, knowing you're nourishing your body with every delicious forkful.

Recipe 23: Pumpkin Risotto

Servings For: (4)

Prepping Time: 20 minutes

Cooking Time: 30 minutes

Difficulty: Medium

Discover the warmth and comfort of Pumpkin Risotto, a perfect addition to your anti-inflammatory dinner recipes. This dish blends creamy arborio rice with the earthy sweetness of pumpkin, creating a meal that's not only delicious but also beneficial for your health.

Preparation Steps

- In a large pan, heat olive oil over medium heat. Add onion and garlic, sautéing until translucent.
- Stir in the arborio rice, ensuring each grain is coated with oil.
- Add diced pumpkin and cook for 5 minutes.
- Gradually add vegetable broth, one cup at a time, stirring continuously until the liquid is absorbed before adding more.
- Once the rice is tender and creamy, remove from heat. Stir in Parmesan cheese, salt, and pepper.
- Garnish with fresh parsley and serve warm.

Ingredients

- 1 cup arborio rice
- 2 cups diced pumpkin
- One onion, finely chopped
- Three cloves garlic, minced
- 4 cups vegetable broth
- 1/2 cup grated Parmesan cheese
- 2 tbsp olive oil
- Salt and pepper to taste
- Fresh parsley for garnish

Nutritional Facts: (Per serving)

- Calories: 350
- Protein: 10g
- Carbohydrates: 60g
- Fiber: 4g
- Sugar: 5g
- Fat: 8g

In conclusion, this Pumpkin Risotto not only pleases your taste buds but also offers anti-inflammatory benefits, making it a smart choice for a health-conscious diet. Its rich flavors and creamy texture make it an ideal comfort food for chilly evenings or a festive autumn meal.

Recipe 24: Rack of Lamb Chops With Couscous

Servings For: (04)

Prepping Time: 20 minutes

Cooking Time: 30 minutes

Difficulty: Intermediate

Embark on a culinary journey with this exquisite Rack of Lamb Chops with Couscous, a perfect addition to your anti-inflammatory dinner repertoire. This recipe artfully combines the rich flavor of lamb with the light, fluffy texture of couscous, creating a harmonious blend of taste and health benefits.

Preparation Steps

- Preheat the oven to 375°F (190°C).
- Season the lamb with salt, pepper, rosemary, and garlic.
- Heat olive oil over medium heat and sear the lamb on all sides.
- Transfer the lamb to the oven and roast for 20 minutes.
- Meanwhile, bring the vegetable broth to a boil, add couscous, cover, and remove from heat. Let it sit for 5 minutes.
- Fluff the couscous with a fork, then mix in tomatoes, parsley, lemon zest, and juice.
- Once the lamb is cooked, rest for 5 minutes before slicing.
- Serve the lamb chops with couscous.

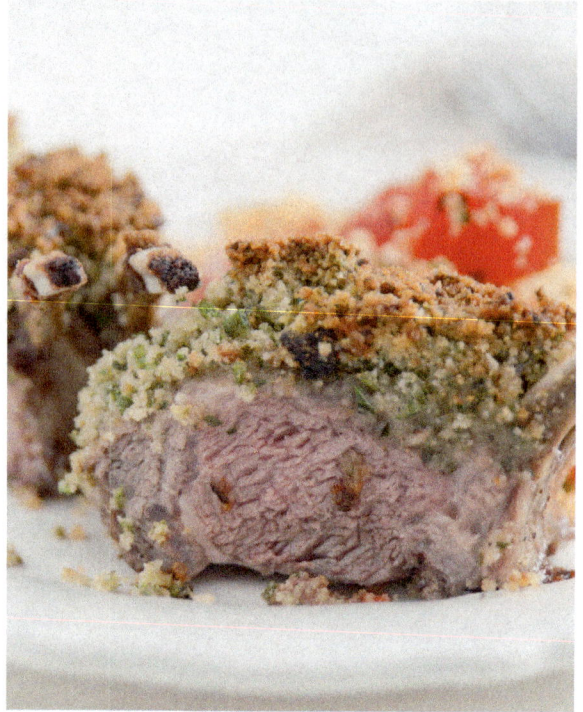

Ingredients

- One rack of lamb, trimmed
- Two tablespoons of olive oil
- One teaspoon of rosemary, minced
- Two cloves garlic, minced
- Salt and pepper, to taste
- 1 cup couscous
- 1 1/2 cups vegetable broth
- 1/2 cup cherry tomatoes, halved
- 1/4 cup parsley, chopped
- One lemon, zest and juice

Nutritional Facts: (Per serving)

- Calories: 450
- Protein: 35g
- Carbohydrates: 35g
- Fat: 20g
- Fiber: 3g
- Sugar: 2g
- Sodium: 300mg

Conclude your day with this Rack of Lamb Chops with Couscous, the epitome of a healthy yet luxurious dining experience. Not only does it tantalize your taste buds, but it also contributes positively to your anti-inflammatory diet. Let this dish testify to how indulgence and well-being coexist on your dinner table.

Recipe 25: Cauliflower Pizza Crust With Pesto

Servings For: (02)

Prepping Time: 20 minutes

Cooking Time: 30 minutes

Difficulty: Medium

Cauliflower pizza crust with pesto is a delectable and healthy twist to your traditional pizza. This anti-inflammatory dinner recipe is delicious and packed with nutrients, making it an ideal meal for those looking to enjoy pizza in a healthier way.

Preparation Steps

- Preheat oven to 400°F (200°C).
- Grate cauliflower and steam until soft.
- Squeeze out excess water from cauliflower.
- Mix cauliflower with almond flour, egg, salt, and pepper.
- Spread the mixture on a baking sheet to form a crust.
- Bake for 20 minutes until golden.
- Add mozzarella and toppings.
- Bake for another 10 minutes.
- Drizzle pesto sauce over the pizza.

Ingredients

- One large head of cauliflower
- 1/4 cup almond flour
- One egg
- 1/2 tsp salt
- 1/4 tsp black pepper
- 1 cup shredded mozzarella
- 1/2 cup pesto sauce
- Toppings of choice (vegetables, chicken, etc.)

Nutritional Facts: (Per serving)

- Calories: 320
- Protein: 15g
- Carbohydrates: 18g
- Fat: 22g
- Fiber: 5g
- Sugar: 4g

This cauliflower pizza crust with pesto offers a delightful and healthier alternative to traditional pizza. It's perfect for a cozy night in or a casual dinner party. It is delicious and brings the added benefits of being anti-inflammatory, making it a guilt-free indulgence for pizza lovers.

Recipe 26: Tofu Stir Fry With Carrot, Broccoli and Cashews

Servings For: (04)

Prepping Time: 15 minutes

Cooking Time: 20 minutes

Difficulty: Easy

Discover the vibrant flavors and health benefits of "Tofu Stir Fry with Carrot, Broccoli, and Cashews." This delightful dish, part of our Anti-Inflammatory Dinners collection, combines the nutritional power of tofu with the crunch of fresh vegetables and cashews, creating a meal that's as nourishing as it is delicious. It's perfect for anyone seeking a wholesome yet easy-to-prepare dinner option.

Preparation Steps

- Press tofu to remove excess moisture, then cube.
- Heat sesame oil in a large pan over medium heat.
- Add garlic and ginger, sautéing until fragrant.
- Add tofu and cook until golden brown on all sides.
- Add carrots and broccoli, stir-frying until tender.
- Toss in cashews, drizzle with soy sauce, and season with salt and pepper.
- Cook for another 5 minutes, stirring occasionally.

Ingredients

- One block of firm tofu cubed
- Two carrots, sliced
- One head of broccoli, cut into florets
- 1/2 cup cashews, unsalted
- Two tablespoons of soy sauce
- One tablespoon of sesame oil
- One teaspoon of ginger, minced
- Two garlic cloves, minced
- Salt and pepper, to taste

Nutritional Facts: (Per serving)

- Calories: 200
- Protein: 12g
- Carbohydrates: 18g
- Fat: 10g
- Fiber: 4g
- Sugar: 3g

As you savor each bite of this Tofu Stir Fry with Carrot, Broccoli, and Cashews, know that you're not just enjoying a delicious meal but also taking a step towards better health. This dish, rich in anti-inflammatory ingredients, is a testament to the power of food as medicine. It's a culinary experience that nourishes your body and soul, perfect for any night of the week.

Recipe 27: Grilled Portobello Mushroom

Servings For:
(04)

Prepping Time:
15 minutes

Cooking Time:
8 minutes

Difficulty:
Easy

Embark on a culinary journey with this delicious Grilled Portobello Mushroom recipe, a perfect addition to your anti-inflammatory dinner menu. Savor the earthy flavors and rich, meaty texture of portobellos, skillfully grilled to perfection. Ideal for health-conscious diners, this dish offers a delightful blend of taste and nutrition, catering to vegetarians and mushroom enthusiasts alike.

Preparation Steps

- Clean the portobello mushrooms gently with a damp cloth.
- Mix olive oil, garlic, thyme, rosemary, salt, and pepper in a small bowl.
- Brush the mushrooms with the oil mixture, ensuring they coat them evenly.
- Preheat the grill to medium heat.
- Place mushrooms on the grill, cap side down, and grill for about 4 minutes.
- Flip the mushrooms and grill for another 4 minutes or until tender.
- Drizzle balsamic vinegar over the mushrooms before serving.

Ingredients

- Four large portobello mushrooms, stems removed
- Two tablespoons of olive oil
- One teaspoon of garlic, minced
- One teaspoon thyme, chopped
- One teaspoon rosemary, chopped
- Salt and pepper to taste
- One tablespoon of balsamic vinegar

Nutritional Facts: (Per serving)

- Calories: 80
- Protein: 2g
- Carbohydrates: 4g
- Fat: 7g
- Sodium: 10mg
- Fiber: 1g

Conclude your day with this delectable Grilled Portobello Mushroom dish, a stellar choice for those seeking a hearty yet healthy meal. Its anti-inflammatory properties, coupled with its delightful flavor profile, make it a must-try. Whether you're a mushroom lover or exploring healthy dinner options, this recipe promises to be a lovely addition to your culinary repertoire.

Recipe 28: Fried Shrimp and Asparagus With Mushrooms

Servings For: (04)

Prepping Time: 15 minutes

Cooking Time: 20 minutes

Difficulty: Medium

Embark on a culinary journey with this delicious Fried Shrimp and Asparagus with Mushrooms recipe, perfect for anyone seeking a wholesome, anti-inflammatory dinner. It's a delightful blend of savory shrimp, crisp asparagus, and earthy mushrooms, creating a dish that's tasty and beneficial for your health.

Preparation Steps

- Heat olive oil in a large skillet over medium heat. Add garlic and sauté until fragrant.
- Add mushrooms and cook until they start to soften.
- Incorporate the asparagus and cook until it's tender but still crisp.
- Add the shrimp, paprika, salt, and pepper. Cook until shrimp are pink and cooked through.
- Serve hot, garnished with lemon wedges.

Ingredients

- 1 lb fresh shrimp, peeled and deveined
- One bunch of asparagus, trimmed and cut into pieces
- 1 cup mushrooms, sliced
- Two cloves garlic, minced
- 2 tbsp olive oil
- 1 tsp paprika
- Salt and pepper, to taste
- One lemon, for garnish

Nutritional Facts: (Per serving)

- Calories: 200
- Protein: 23g
- Carbohydrates: 10g
- Fat: 8g
- Fiber: 3g
- Sugar: 2g

Conclude your day with this delicious and healthful Fried Shrimp and Asparagus with Mushrooms dish. It's a feast for the taste buds and a step towards a healthier lifestyle, thanks to its anti-inflammatory properties. Enjoy this easy-to-make, nutrient-packed meal that's sure to be a hit at any dinner table.

Recipe 29: Baked Cod With Cherry Tomatoes and Thyme

Servings For: (4)

Prepping Time: 15 minutes

Cooking Time: 20 minutes

Difficulty: Easy

Embark on a culinary journey with "Baked Cod with Cherry Tomatoes and Thyme," a dish perfect for those seeking anti-inflammatory dinner options. This recipe combines the delicate flavors of cod with the zest of cherry tomatoes and the aromatic touch of thyme, creating a meal that's healthy and a delight to the senses.

Preparation Steps

- Preheat your oven to 375°F (190°C).
- Arrange cod fillets in a baking dish.
- Toss cherry tomatoes with olive oil, garlic, and thyme. Season with salt and pepper.
- Spread the tomato mixture around the cod in the word.
- Bake for 20 minutes or until the cod is cooked through.
- Serve with lemon wedges and enjoy.

Ingredients

- Four cod fillets
- 2 cups cherry tomatoes, halved
- Three tablespoons olive oil
- Two cloves garlic, minced
- One tablespoon of fresh thyme, chopped
- Salt and pepper, to taste
- Lemon wedges for serving

Nutritional Facts: (Per serving)

- Calories: 200
- Protein: 22g
- Carbohydrates: 6g
- Fat: 10g
- Sodium: 70mg
- Fiber: 1g

As you savor each bite of Baked Cod with Cherry Tomatoes and Thyme, revel in the knowledge that you're nourishing your body with anti-inflammatory goodness. This simple yet elegant dish is not just a meal but a celebration of healthy and delicious flavors that will surely please your palate and contribute to your well-being.

Recipe 30: Kebab - Grilled Meat and Vegetables

Servings For: (4)

Prepping Time: 20 minutes

Cooking Time: 15 minutes

Difficulty: Easy

Welcome to this delicious journey, where we explore the art of making Kebabs – a perfect blend of grilled meat and vegetables. Not only is it a treat for your taste buds, but it's also an excellent choice for an anti-inflammatory dinner. Let's dive into this simple yet flavorful recipe.

Preparation Steps

- Mix the olive oil, lemon juice, turmeric, paprika, garlic, salt, and pepper in a large bowl.
- Add the meat and vegetables to the bowl and marinate for at least 30 minutes.
- Thread the meat and vegetables onto skewers.
- Preheat the grill to medium-high heat.
- Grill the kebabs for 7-8 minutes on each side or until the meat is cooked to your liking.
- Serve hot with your choice of side dishes.

Ingredients

- 500g lean meat (chicken, beef, or lamb), cut into cubes
- One bell pepper cut into pieces
- One zucchini, sliced
- One red onion, cut into wedges
- Two tablespoons of olive oil
- One teaspoon turmeric
- One teaspoon paprika
- Salt and pepper to taste
- Two cloves of garlic, minced
- Juice of 1 lemon

Nutritional Facts: (Per serving)

- Calories: 250
- Protein: 26g
- Carbohydrates: 12g
- Fat: 10g
- Fiber: 3g
- Sugar: 5g
- Sodium: 120mg

As we conclude this recipe, you're now equipped to create a healthy and delicious meal that satisfies your hunger and contributes positively to your overall health. With their anti-inflammatory properties, these kebabs are more than just a meal; they're a step towards a healthier lifestyle. Enjoy your cooking and savor every bite!

Recipe 31: Greek Yoghurt With Honey and Walnuts

Servings For:
(02)

Prepping Time:
5 minutes

Cooking Time:
0 minutes

Difficulty:
Easy

Greek Yoghurt with Honey and Walnuts is a soothing, nutritious, anti-inflammatory midnight snack. Perfect for those late-night cravings, it combines the creamy texture of Greek yogurt with the sweetness of honey and the crunch of walnuts. This simple yet delightful dish is delicious and packed with health benefits, making it an ideal choice for a quick and easy snack.

Preparation Steps

- In a serving bowl, spoon the Greek yogurt.
- Drizzle the honey evenly over the yogurt.
- Sprinkle the chopped walnuts on top.
- Add a pinch of cinnamon for extra flavor (optional).
- Gently mix everything or serve layered.

Ingredients

- 1 cup Greek yogurt
- Two tablespoons honey
- 1/4 cup walnuts, chopped
- A pinch of cinnamon (optional

Nutritional Facts: (Per serving)

- Calories: 150
- Protein: 8g
- Carbohydrates: 18g
- Fat: 7g
- Sugar: 12g
- Fiber: 1g

Greek Yoghurt with Honey and Walnuts is an effortless, satisfying snack perfect for a quiet night. Its anti-inflammatory properties, coupled with its rich flavors and textures, make it a guilt-free treat. Whether you're looking for a healthy snack or a quick dessert, this recipe is a delightful way to indulge your taste buds without compromising your health.

Recipe 32: Baked Apples Stuffed With Walnuts in Sweet Syrup

Servings For: (04)

Prepping Time: 15 minutes

Cooking Time: 30 minutes

Difficulty: Easy

Embark on a delightful culinary journey with "Baked Apples Stuffed with Walnuts in Sweet Syrup," a perfect anti-inflammatory midnight snack that combines the natural sweetness of apples with the nutty crunch of walnuts; all enveloped in a luscious sweet syrup. This simple yet elegant dish is a treat for your taste buds and a healthy choice for late-night cravings.

Preparation Steps

- Preheat your oven to 350°F (175°C).
- Mix the walnuts, honey or maple syrup, cinnamon, nutmeg, and salt in a bowl.
- Stuff each apple with the walnut mixture.
- Place the stuffed apples in a baking dish and pour water around them.
- Bake for 30 minutes or until the apples are tender.
- Serve warm, drizzled with the sweet syrup from the baking dish.

Ingredients

- Four large apples, cored
- 1/2 cup walnuts, chopped
- 1/4 cup honey or maple syrup
- 1/2 teaspoon ground cinnamon
- 1/4 teaspoon ground nutmeg
- 1/2 cup water
- A pinch of salt

Nutritional Facts: (Per serving)

- Calories: 210
- Protein: 2g
- Carbohydrates: 35g
- Fat: 8g
- Fiber: 5g
- Sugar: 28g

In conclusion, these baked apples stuffed with walnuts in sweet syrup are a delectable treat and a wholesome choice for those late-night hunger pangs. This recipe is a testament to how simple ingredients, when combined thoughtfully, can create an indulgent and healthy dish. Enjoy this delightful snack without guilt, and let it be your go-to recipe for a satisfying, anti-inflammatory midnight treat.

Recipe 33: Turmeric Golden Milk Latte With Cinnamon and Honey

Servings For: (02)

Prepping Time: 10 minutes

Cooking Time: 5 minutes

Difficulty: Easy

Indulge in the soothing warmth of a Turmeric Golden Milk Latte with Cinnamon and Honey. This anti-inflammatory midnight snack is delicious and beneficial for your health. It's a comforting blend of spices and sweetness that calms you before bedtime.

Preparation Steps

- Combine almond milk, turmeric, cinnamon, and ginger in a small saucepan. Heat over medium flame.
- Stir continuously to prevent clumping and ensure even heating.
- Once hot (but not boiling), remove from heat and strain to remove ginger pieces.
- Stir in honey and a pinch of black pepper.
- Pour into cups and serve warm.

Ingredients

- 2 cups of almond milk
- 1 tsp of turmeric powder
- ½ tsp of ground cinnamon
- 1 tbsp of honey (or to taste)
- A pinch of black pepper (to enhance turmeric absorption)
- 1 tsp of grated ginger

Nutritional Facts: (Per serving)

- Calories: 120
- Protein: 1g
- Carbohydrates: 18g
- Fat: 4.5g
- Sugar: 12g
- Dietary Fiber: 1g

Wrap up your day with this Turmeric Golden Milk Latte. Its anti-inflammatory properties and soothing flavors make it an ideal nighttime treat. It is not just a snack; it's a gentle embrace for your well-being, ensuring a peaceful night's rest.

Recipe 34: Strawberry Oatmeal Coconut Milk Smoothie

Servings For:
(02)

Prepping Time:
10 minutes

Cooking Time:
0 minutes

Difficulty:
Easy

Embark on a culinary adventure with the "Strawberry Oatmeal Coconut Milk Smoothie," a delightful blend perfect for those seeking a delicious and anti-inflammatory midnight snack. This recipe not only tantalizes your taste buds but also offers health benefits, making it an ideal choice for a nutritious late-night treat.

Preparation Steps

- Rinse the strawberries and remove the stems.
- Combine strawberries, rolled oats, coconut milk, honey (if using), vanilla extract, and cinnamon in a blender.
- Blend until smooth, adding more coconut milk if needed for desired consistency.
- Taste and adjust sweetness, if necessary.
- Pour into glasses and serve immediately.

Ingredients

- 1 cup fresh strawberries
- 1/2 cup rolled oats
- 1 cup coconut milk
- One tablespoon honey (optional)
- 1/2 teaspoon vanilla extract
- A pinch of cinnamon

Nutritional Facts: (Per serving)

- Calories: 200
- Protein: 3g
- Carbohydrates: 28g
- Fat: 8g
- Dietary Fiber: 4g
- Sugars: 12g

Conclude your day with this Strawberry Oatmeal Coconut Milk Smoothie, a soothing and nourishing midnight snack that's simple to prepare and packed with anti-inflammatory benefits. This smoothie is a treat for your taste buds and a healthful indulgence to enhance your well-being.

Recipe 35: Pumpkin Spice Latte

Servings For:
(02)

Prepping Time:
10 minutes

Cooking Time:
5 minutes

Difficulty:
Easy

Indulge in a Pumpkin Spice Latte's warm, comforting embrace, a perfect anti-inflammatory midnight snack. This delectable treat combines the soothing flavors of pumpkin and spices, creating a calming beverage to unwind with before bed.

Preparation Steps

- In a saucepan, combine milk, pumpkin puree, and sugar. Heat over medium heat, but do not boil.
- Remove from heat and stir in vanilla, pumpkin pie spice, and coffee.
- If desired, pour into mugs and top with whipped cream and a sprinkle of pumpkin pie spice.
- Serve warm and enjoy your cozy, anti-inflammatory treat.

Ingredients

- 2 cups of milk (dairy or plant-based)
- Two tablespoons of pumpkin puree
- 1-2 tablespoons sugar (to taste)
- One tablespoon of vanilla extract
- 1/2 teaspoon pumpkin pie spice
- 1/2 cup strong brewed coffee or espresso
- Whipped cream for topping (optional)

Nutritional Facts: (Per serving)

- Calories: 150
- Protein: 5g
- Carbohydrates: 24g
- Fat: 3g
- Sodium: 95mg
- Sugar: 20g

Savor each sip of your Pumpkin Spice Latte as it warms your soul and eases your mind. Not only is it delicious, but its anti-inflammatory properties also make it a healthy choice for late-night snacks. Let this latte be your sweet companion in the quiet night hours.

Recipe 36: Roasted Red Pepper Hummus With Pita Bread

Servings For: (04)

Prepping Time: 15 minutes

Cooking Time: 5 minutes

Difficulty: Easy

Enjoy the rich flavors of Roasted Red Pepper Hummus with Pita Bread, a delectable and healthy anti-inflammatory midnight snack. This dish combines the creamy texture of hummus with the sweet and smoky taste of roasted red peppers, making it a perfect choice for a late-night treat that's both satisfying and nutritious.

Preparation Steps

- Combine chickpeas, roasted red peppers, garlic, tahini, lemon juice, olive oil, cumin, salt, and pepper in a food processor.
- Blend until smooth, scraping down the sides as needed.
- Taste and adjust seasoning if necessary.
- Serve the hummus in a bowl, drizzled with olive oil.
- Warm the pita bread in an oven or skillet, and cut into wedges.
- Serve the pita wedges alongside the hummus for dipping.

Ingredients

- One can of chickpeas, drained and rinsed
- Two roasted red peppers, homemade or store-bought
- Two cloves garlic, minced
- Two tablespoons tahini
- Juice of 1 lemon
- Two tablespoons of olive oil
- 1/2 teaspoon ground cumin
- Salt and pepper, to taste
- Pita bread for serving

Nutritional Facts: (Per serving)

- Calories: 150
- Protein: 6g
- Carbohydrates: 20g
- Dietary Fiber: 4g
- Sugars: 2g
- Fat: 7g

Wrap up your day with this Roasted Red Pepper Hummus with Pita Bread, a delightful snack that's tasty and beneficial for your health. Its anti-inflammatory properties make it an ideal choice for a nutritious midnight snack. Whether you're looking for a quick bite or a healthy treat, this recipe will satisfy your cravings without the guilt.

Recipe 37: Cottage Cheese With Fresh Pineapple and Raspberries

Servings For:
(02)

Prepping Time:
10 minutes

Cooking Time:
0 minutes

Difficulty:
Easy

Discover the perfect anti-inflammatory midnight snack with our delightful Cottage Cheese with Fresh Pineapple and Raspberries recipe. Packed with refreshing flavors and nutritional benefits, this dish is ideal for a light, healthy treat before bed.

Preparation Steps

- In a medium bowl, combine the cottage cheese with honey and cinnamon.
- Gently fold the diced pineapple and raspberries, ensuring the berries are not crushed.
- Divide the mixture into two serving bowls.
- Refrigerate for 5 minutes if a more relaxed snack is preferred.

Ingredients

- 1 cup low-fat cottage cheese
- 1/2 cup fresh pineapple, diced
- 1/2 cup fresh raspberries
- One tablespoon honey (optional)
- A pinch of cinnamon (optional)

Nutritional Facts: (Per serving)

- Calories: 150
- Protein: 15g
- Carbohydrates: 20g
- Fiber: 2g
- Sugar: 15g
- Fat: 2g

End your day on a delicious and healthful note with this easy-to-prepare cottage cheese snack. Bursting with the sweetness of fresh pineapple and raspberries, it's satisfying and an excellent choice for those late-night cravings, providing essential nutrients without guilt.

Recipe 38: Hummus and Vegetable With Tortillas

Servings For:
(02)

Prepping Time:
15 minutes

Cooking Time:
5 minutes

Difficulty:
Easy

Indulge in the perfect blend of health and taste with "Hummus and Vegetable with Tortillas," a delectable anti-inflammatory midnight snack recipe. This easy-to-make dish combines the creamy richness of hummus with the crunch of fresh vegetables, all wrapped in a soft tortilla, making it an ideal choice for a late-night treat that's both nutritious and satisfying.

Preparation Steps

- Lay out the tortillas on a flat surface.
- Spread a generous layer of hummus over each tortilla.
- Evenly distribute the cucumber, carrot, bell pepper, onion, and spinach on the hummus.
- Season with salt and pepper.
- Carefully roll up the tortillas, tucking in the sides as you go.
- Slice each roll into halves or bite-sized pieces.
- Serve immediately or refrigerate for a chilled snack.

Ingredients

- Two large tortillas
- 1 cup hummus
- 1/2 cucumber, thinly sliced
- One carrot, grated
- One bell pepper, thinly sliced
- 1/4 red onion, thinly sliced
- A handful of spinach leaves
- Salt and pepper, to taste

Nutritional Facts: (Per serving)

- Calories: 320
- Protein: 10g
- Fiber: 6g
- Fat: 9g
- Sodium: 490mg

Conclude your day on a high note with this delightful Hummus and Vegetable with Tortillas snack. Not only does it satiate your late-night cravings, it also provides a burst of nutrients that combat inflammation. This recipe is a testament to how simple ingredients can be transformed into a gastronomic delight, proving that healthy eating doesn't have to be a chore, even at midnight.

Recipe 39: Coconut Vegan Yogurt Coconut With Banana Chips

Servings For: (02)

Prepping Time: 10 minutes

Cooking Time: 0 minutes

Difficulty: Easy

Embark on a culinary adventure with our Coconut Vegan Yogurt topped with Banana Chips, a perfect anti-inflammatory midnight snack. This delightful recipe offers a harmonious blend of creamy coconut yogurt and the lovely crunch of banana chips, promising a guilt-free indulgence that satiates your late-night cravings while providing health benefits.

Preparation Steps

- In a bowl, gently stir the coconut yogurt to ensure a smooth consistency.
- Sprinkle chia seeds over the yogurt and mix well.
- Add a pinch of cinnamon and honey (if using) to the yogurt and blend.
- Carefully top the yogurt with crushed banana chips.
- Garnish with fresh mint leaves.
- Serve immediately or chill for a refreshing snack.

Ingredients

- 1 cup coconut yogurt
- ½ cup banana chips, crushed
- One tablespoon of chia seeds
- One teaspoon of honey (optional for sweetness)
- A pinch of ground cinnamon
- Fresh mint leaves for garnish

Nutritional Facts: (Per serving)

- Calories: 150
- Protein: 3g
- Carbohydrates: 20g
- Fat: 7g
- Sugar: 10g (natural sugars)
- Dietary Fiber: 2g

Conclude your day sweetly with this Coconut Vegan Yogurt with Banana Chips. This recipe satisfies your midnight snack cravings and supports your wellness journey with its anti-inflammatory properties. Easy to prepare and utterly delicious, it's the perfect way to treat yourself without any dietary guilt. Enjoy this delightful snack and feel good about your choice!

Recipe 40: Guacamole With Fresh Green Chilli With Carrot and Celery

Servings For: (02)

Prepping Time: 15 minutes

Cooking Time: 0 minutes

Difficulty: Easy

Embark on a culinary journey with this delectable Guacamole with Fresh Green chili, Carrot, and Celery - a perfect anti-inflammatory midnight snack. Packed with flavors and health benefits, it's a delightful treat for those late-night cravings.

Preparation Steps

- Cut avocados in half, remove the pit, and scoop the flesh into a bowl.
- Mash the avocado with a fork to your desired consistency.
- Add the chopped green chili, grated Carrot, diced Celery, and lime juice to the mashed avocado.
- Mix in the chopped cilantro and season with salt and pepper.
- Stir everything together until well combined.
- Taste and adjust seasoning if necessary.

Ingredients

- Two ripe avocados
- One fresh green chili, finely chopped
- One small Carrot, grated
- Two celery stalks, finely diced
- Juice of 1 lime
- 2 tbsp chopped cilantro
- Salt and pepper to taste

Nutritional Facts: (Per serving)

- Calories: 250
- Protein: 3g
- Carbohydrates: 15g
- Dietary Fiber: 7g
- Sugars: 2g
- Fat: 22g
- Saturated Fat: 3.5g
- Sodium: 10mg

Wrap up your night with this soothing and nutritious Guacamole with Fresh Green Chilli, Carrot, and Celery. Not only does it satisfy your midnight hunger pangs, but it also offers a burst of flavors and health benefits. Enjoy this quick and easy snack guilt-free!

Chapter 05 : Salads Recipes

Recipe 41: Kale Avocado Pine Nuts Cheese Salad

Servings For: (04)

Prepping Time: 15 minutes

Cooking Time: 0 minutes

Difficulty: Easy

Embark on a journey to wellness with this Kale Avocado Pine Nuts Cheese Salad, a delightful mix that's not only delicious but also packed with anti-inflammatory benefits. This recipe seamlessly blends the bold flavors and textures of kale, creamy avocado, crunchy pine nuts, and decadent cheese, creating a salad that's as nutritious as it is tasty.

Preparation Steps

- Combine the chopped kale, diced avocados, and toasted pine nuts in a large salad bowl.
- Add the shaved Parmesan cheese to the bowl.
- In a small bowl, whisk together the olive oil and lemon juice. Season with salt and pepper.
- Pour the dressing over the salad and toss gently to coat all ingredients evenly.
- Let the salad sit for 5-10 minutes to allow the flavors to meld together before serving.

Ingredients

- One large bunch of fresh kale stems removed and leaves chopped
- Two ripe avocados, diced
- 1/2 cup of pine nuts, toasted
- 1/2 cup of shaved Parmesan cheese
- 1/4 cup of extra-virgin olive oil
- Two tablespoons of fresh lemon juice
- Salt and black pepper, to taste

Nutritional Facts: (Per serving)

- Calories: 300
- Protein: 8g
- Fat: 25g
- Carbohydrates: 15g
- Fiber: 6g
- Sugar: 2g

Conclude your meal with a sense of accomplishment, knowing you've nourished your body with a salad that's not just a treat for your taste buds but also a boon for your health. The Kale Avocado Pine Nuts Cheese Salad is a testament to the idea that eating well can be both simple and delicious, making it a perfect addition to your collection of anti-inflammatory recipes.

Recipe 42 : Spinach Strawberry Nuts Salad

Servings For:
(4)

Prepping Time:
15 minutes

Cooking Time:
0 minutes

Difficulty:
Easy

Spinach Strawberry Nuts Salad, a delightful blend of fresh spinach, sweet strawberries, and crunchy nuts, offers a perfect combination of flavors and textures. Rich in anti-inflammatory properties, this salad is as nutritious as it is delicious, making it a great addition to any meal or as a standalone dish.

Preparation Steps

- Rinse spinach leaves and pat dry.
- Slice strawberries and set aside.
- In a large bowl, combine spinach, strawberries, and nuts.
- Drizzle olive oil and balsamic vinegar over the salad.
- Add feta cheese, salt, and pepper to taste.
- Toss gently to combine all ingredients evenly.

Ingredients

- 2 cups fresh spinach leaves
- 1 cup sliced strawberries
- 1/2 cup mixed nuts (almonds, walnuts, pecans)
- 1/4 cup crumbled feta cheese
- Two tablespoons of olive oil
- One tablespoon of balsamic vinegar
- Salt and pepper, to taste

Nutritional Facts: (Per serving)

- Calories: 150
- Protein: 4g
- Carbohydrates: 10g
- Fat: 11g
- Dietary Fiber: 3g
- Sugars: 4g

This Spinach Strawberry Nuts Salad is a testament to the beauty of simple, fresh ingredients coming together to create a flavorful and healthy dish. Its anti-inflammatory benefits and easy preparation make it an ideal choice for a quick lunch or a refreshing side dish. Enjoy every bite's delightful interplay of sweet, savory, and crunchy!

Recipe 43 : Quinoa Salad With Roasted Butternut Squash

Servings For: (4)

Prepping Time: 15 minutes

Cooking Time: 30 minutes

Difficulty: Easy

This refreshing and nutritious quinoa salad, featuring roasted butternut squash, is a perfect blend of flavors and textures. It's a standout recipe in the realm of anti-inflammatory salads, offering a healthy and delicious meal option.

Preparation Steps

- Preheat the oven to 400°F (200°C). Toss butternut squash with olive oil, cinnamon, salt, and pepper. Roast for 25-30 minutes until tender.
- Cook quinoa according to package instructions.
- Combine roasted squash, cooked quinoa, red onion, walnuts, and cranberries in a large bowl.
- Whisk together the ingredients for the dressing and pour over the salad. Toss to combine.

Ingredients

- 1 cup quinoa
- 2 cups diced butternut squash
- 1/2 cup diced red onion
- 1/4 cup chopped walnuts
- 1/4 cup dried cranberries
- Two tablespoons of olive oil
- One teaspoon ground cinnamon
- Salt and pepper to taste
- For the dressing: 3 tablespoons balsamic vinegar, one tablespoon honey, 1/2 teaspoon minced garlic, salt, and pepper

Nutritional Facts: (Per serving)

- Calories: 315
- Protein: 8g
- Carbohydrates: 53g
- Fat: 10g
- Fiber: 7g
- Sugar: 10g
- Sodium: 30mg

This quinoa salad with roasted butternut squash is a feast for the taste buds and a powerhouse of anti-inflammatory benefits. It's an ideal dish for those looking to enjoy a flavorful yet health-conscious meal, perfectly embodying the essence of nutritious eating with a gourmet twist.

Recipe 44 : Beetroot, Cheese, Arugula and Walnuts Salad

Servings For: (04)

Prepping Time: 15 minutes

Cooking Time: 0 minutes

Difficulty: Easy

Indulge in the vibrant flavors of our Beetroot, Cheese, Arugula, and walnut salad. This anti-inflammatory recipe is a feast for the eyes and a powerhouse of nutrients. Perfect for health-conscious food lovers, it combines the earthy sweetness of beetroot with the creaminess of cheese, the peppery taste of arugula, and the crunch of walnuts.

Preparation Steps

- In a large mixing bowl, combine the sliced beetroots and arugula leaves.
- Add the crumbled cheese and chopped walnuts to the bowl.
- Whisk together olive oil, balsamic vinegar, salt, and pepper in a small bowl.
- Pour the dressing over the salad and gently toss to coat evenly.
- Serve immediately or chill in the refrigerator for an hour before serving.

Ingredients

- Three medium-sized beetroots peeled and thinly sliced
- 1 cup arugula leaves, washed and dried
- ½ cup crumbled feta cheese or goat cheese
- ¼ cup walnuts, chopped
- Two tablespoons of olive oil
- One tablespoon of balsamic vinegar
- Salt and pepper, to taste

Nutritional Facts: (Per serving)

- Calories: 180
- Protein: 5g
- Carbohydrates: 12g
- Fat: 12g
- Dietary Fiber: 3g
- Sugar: 7g

Savor the delightful textures and flavors in this Beetroot, Cheese, Arugula, and walnut salad. Not only does it bring a burst of color to your table, but it's also loaded with anti-inflammatory benefits. Easy to prepare and irresistibly tasty, this salad is perfect for a healthy, quick meal or a fancy side dish for your gatherings.

Recipe 45 : Creamy Broccoli Slaw

Servings For: (04)

Prepping Time: 15 minutes

Cooking Time: 0 minutes

Difficulty: Easy

Creamy broccoli slaw, a delightful anti-inflammatory salad, is an exquisite blend o crunchy carrots and tangy dressing. This salad is delicious and packed with nutrients tha help reduce inflammation.

Preparation Steps

- Combine shredded broccoli stems, carrot, and red onion in a large bowl.
- Whisk together mayonnaise, apple cider vinegar, and honey in a separate small bowl.
- Pour the dressing over the vegetable mixture and toss until well coated.
- Season with salt and pepper to taste.
- Refrigerate for at least 30 minutes before serving to allow flavors to meld.

Ingredients

- 3 cups of shredded broccoli stems
- One large carrot, shredded
- 1/4 cup red onion, finely chopped
- 1/2 cup mayonnaise (preferably low-fat)
- Two tablespoons of apple cider vinegar
- One tablespoon honey
- Salt and pepper, to taste

Nutritional Facts: (Per serving)

- Calories: 190
- Fat: 15g
- Carbohydrates: 13g
- Protein: 2g
- Fiber: 3g
- Sugar: 7g

This creamy broccoli slaw is a perfect side dish for any meal and a great way to enjoy the benefits of anti-inflammatory foods. Its combination of flavors and textures makes it a hit at gatherings or as a healthy lunch option. Enjoy this delicious salad and embrace a healthier lifestyle.

Recipe 46 : Lentil Salad With Cucumber, Bell Pepper and Coriander Leaves on Rustic

Servings For: (04)

Prepping Time: 15 minutes

Cooking Time: 20 minutes

Difficulty: Easy

Lentil salad with cucumber, bell pepper, and coriander leaves is a delightful dish with flavors and health benefits. Ideal for anyone looking for a nutritious and anti-inflammatory option, this salad is both delicious and easy to prepare.

Preparation Steps

- In a medium pot, bring lentils and water to a boil. Reduce heat and simmer for 20 minutes or until lentils are tender.
- Drain lentils and let them cool.
- Combine cooled lentils, cucumber, bell pepper, and coriander leaves in a large bowl.
- Whisk together olive oil, lemon juice, salt, and pepper in a small bowl.
- Pour the dressing over the salad and toss gently to combine.
- Serve chilled or at room temperature.

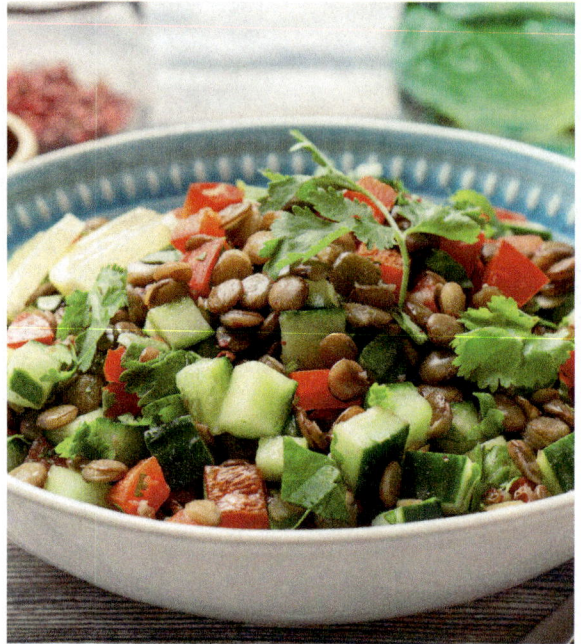

Ingredients

- 1 cup lentils, rinsed
- 2 cups water
- One large cucumber, diced
- One bell pepper, finely chopped
- A handful of fresh coriander leaves chopped
- Three tablespoons olive oil
- Two tablespoons of lemon juice
- Salt and pepper, to taste

Nutritional Facts: (Per serving)

- Calories: 180
- Protein: 9g
- Dietary Fiber: 8g
- Sugars: 3g
- Vitamin C: 40% DV
- Iron: 15% DV

This lentil salad is more than just a dish; it's a vibrant mix of flavors and nutrients. Perfect as a side or a light main course, it's a testament to how delicious healthy eating can be. Whether you're a salad lover or want to add more anti-inflammatory foods, this recipe is a must-try.

Recipe 47 : Red Cabbage Salad With Apples

Servings For:
(04)

Prepping Time:
15 minutes

Cooking Time:
0 minutes

Difficulty:
Easy

Discover the vibrant flavors of this delicious Red Cabbage Salad with Apples, a perfect addition to your anti-inflammatory diet. Packed with nutrients, it's a simple yet delightful dish that combines the crispness of red cabbage with the sweetness of apples, creating a refreshing balance.

Preparation Steps

- Mix the sliced red cabbage, apples, and red onion in a large bowl.
- Whisk together apple cider vinegar, olive oil, honey, salt, and pepper in a small bowl.
- Pour the dressing over the salad and toss until well combined.
- Let the salad sit for about 10 minutes to marinate.
- Before serving, sprinkle with chopped walnuts and garnish with fresh parsley.

Ingredients

- One medium red cabbage, thinly sliced
- Two red apples, sliced
- 1/4 cup red onion, thinly sliced
- Two tablespoons of apple cider vinegar
- One tablespoon of olive oil
- One teaspoon honey
- Salt and pepper, to taste
- 1/4 cup chopped walnuts (optional)
- Fresh parsley for garnish

Nutritional Facts: (Per serving)

- Calories: 120
- Protein: 2g
- Carbohydrates: 20g
- Dietary Fiber: 4g
- Sugars: 12g
- Fat: 4g
- Sodium: 20mg

Embrace the power of anti-inflammatory eating with this Red Cabbage Salad with Apples. It's not just a salad; it's a celebration of healthful ingredients coming together in a symphony of flavors. Enjoy this delightful dish as a standalone meal or a vibrant side, knowing you're nurturing your body with every bite.

Recipe 48: Salad With Pear and Walnuts

Servings For:
(4)

Prepping Time:
15 minutes

Cooking Time:
0 minutes

Difficulty:
Easy

Discover the perfect blend of taste and health with our Salad with Pear and Walnuts recipe. This anti-inflammatory salad is delicious and packed with nutrients that promote well-being.

Preparation Steps

- Combine mixed greens, sliced pears, and chopped walnuts in a large bowl.
- Add crumbled feta cheese to the salad.
- Whisk together olive oil, balsamic vinegar, salt, and pepper in a small bowl.
- Drizzle the dressing over the salad and toss gently to combine.

Ingredients

- Two ripe pears, sliced
- 1 cup walnuts, chopped
- 4 cups mixed greens
- 1/2 cup crumbled feta cheese
- 1/4 cup extra virgin olive oil
- Two tablespoons of balsamic vinegar
- Salt and pepper to taste

Nutritional Facts: (Per serving)

- Calories: 290
- Protein: 6g
- Fat: 24g
- Carbohydrates: 17g
- Dietary Fiber: 4g

Savor the flavors of freshness with this Salad with Pear and Walnuts. Ideal for those seeking a healthy, anti-inflammatory diet, this recipe is a testament to how simple ingredients can create a symphony of flavors. Enjoy this salad as a stand-alone meal or a complement to your main dish.

Recipe 49: Carrot and Apple Salad With Raisins, Yogurt and Herbs

Servings For: (04)

Prepping Time: 15 minutes

Cooking Time: 0 minutes

Difficulty: Easy

Enjoy the flavors and health benefits of this Carrot and Apple Salad with Raisins, Yogurt, and Herbs. This anti-inflammatory recipe is a delightful blend of crunchy carrots, sweet apples, and plump raisins, all brought together with a creamy yogurt dressing. Fresh herbs add a layer of flavor, making this salad a perfect choice for health-conscious foodies

Preparation Steps

- In a large bowl, combine the grated carrots and chopped apples.
- Add the raisins to the bowl.
- Mix the yogurt with the chopped herbs, honey (if using), and a pinch of salt and pepper in a separate small bowl.
- Pour the yogurt dressing over the carrot and apple mixture. Toss well to ensure everything is evenly coated.
- Refrigerate the salad for 30 minutes before serving to allow flavors to meld.

Ingredients

- Two large carrots, grated
- Two apples, cored and chopped
- 1/2 cup raisins
- 1 cup plain yogurt
- A handful of fresh herbs (such as parsley and mint), chopped
- One tablespoon honey (optional)
- Salt and pepper, to taste

Nutritional Facts: (Per serving)

- Calories: 150
- Protein: 3g
- Carbohydrates: 34g
- Fat: 2g
- Dietary Fiber: 4g
- Sugars: 28g

As you savor each spoonful of this Carrot and Apple Salad with Raisins, Yogurt, and Herbs, relish that you're indulging in a dish that's not just delicious but also packed with anti-inflammatory benefits. This simple, refreshing salad is perfect for a quick lunch or as a side dish with dinner, providing a delightful combination of textures and flavors that's sure to please any palate.

Recipe 50: Edamame Salad

Servings For:
(4)

Prepping Time:
5 minutes

Cooking Time:
5 minutes

Difficulty:
Easy

Welcome to the refreshing world of edamame salad, a delightful blend of flavors and nutrients that makes for a perfect anti-inflammatory meal. This salad is delicious and packed with health benefits, making it an ideal choice for those looking to enjoy a nutritious dish.

Preparation Steps

- Combine the cooked edamame, red bell pepper, and red onion in a large bowl.
- Whisk together olive oil, lemon juice, honey, salt, and pepper in a small bowl to create the dressing.
- Pour the sauce over the salad and toss to coat evenly.
- Sprinkle with chopped cilantro and give it a final mix.
- Let the salad sit for about 10 minutes to absorb the flavors before serving.

Ingredients

- 2 cups shelled edamame, cooked and cooled
- One red bell pepper, finely chopped
- 1/2 cup red onion, finely chopped
- 1/4 cup fresh cilantro, chopped
- Two tablespoons of olive oil
- Two tablespoons of lemon juice
- One teaspoon honey
- Salt and pepper to taste

Nutritional Facts: (Per serving)

- Calories: 180
- Protein: 12g
- Fiber: 5g
- Fat: 9g (Saturated Fat: 1g)
- Sodium: 150mg

In conclusion, this edamame salad is more than just a meal; it's a vibrant, health-boosting dish that brings together taste and wellness. Whether you're seeking an anti-inflammatory diet or a delicious salad, this recipe will surely please your palate and contribute to your overall health

Chapter 06 : Soup Recipes

Recipe 51: Tomato Soup

Servings For:
(04)

Prepping Time:
15 minutes

Cooking Time:
30 minutes

Difficulty:
Easy

Experience the warmth and comfort of homemade tomato soup, a perfect choice for those seeking anti-inflammatory recipes. This nutritious soup is delicious and aids in reducing inflammation, making it a wholesome addition to your diet.

Preparation Steps

- Heat olive oil in a large pot over medium heat.
- Add onions and garlic, and sauté until soft.
- Mix in carrots and cook for 5 minutes.
- Stir in tomatoes, basil, oregano, salt, and pepper.
- Pour in vegetable broth and bring to a boil.
- Reduce heat and simmer for 20 minutes.
- Blend the soup until smooth.
- Taste and adjust seasoning as needed.

Ingredients

- 4 cups ripe tomatoes, chopped
- One onion, finely chopped
- Two cloves garlic, minced
- One carrot, diced
- 2 tbsp olive oil
- 1 tsp dried basil
- 1 tsp dried oregano
- Salt and pepper to taste
- 4 cups vegetable broth

Nutritional Facts: (Per serving)

- Calories: 90
- Protein: 2g
- Carbohydrates: 12g
- Fat: 4g
- Sodium: 210mg
- Fiber: 3g

Savor this classic tomato soup's rich, tangy flavors, elevated with anti-inflammatory properties. It's a delightful way to soothe your body and uplift your spirits. This soup will become a cherished part of your culinary repertoire, ideal for cozy evenings or as a nourishing meal.

Recipe 52: Pumpkin and Carrot Soup

Servings For:
(04)

Prepping Time:
15 minutes

Cooking Time:
45 minutes

Difficulty:
Easy

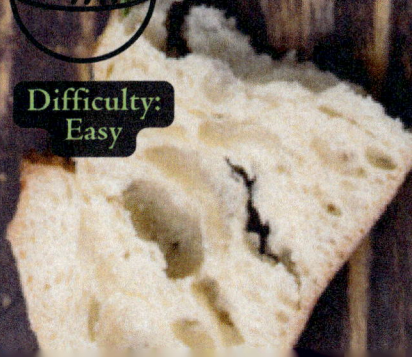

Discover the warmth and healing power of our Pumpkin and Carrot Soup, a delightful blend perfect for soothing the body. This anti-inflammatory recipe promises comfort and a burst of flavors that will surely nourish your soul.

Preparation Steps

- In a large pot, heat olive oil over medium heat. Add onions and garlic, and sauté until translucent.
- Add pumpkin, carrots, ginger, and turmeric. Cook for 5 minutes, stirring occasionally.
- Pour in vegetable broth. Bring to a boil, then reduce heat and simmer for 30 minutes or until vegetables are soft.
- Use an immersion blender to puree the soup until smooth. Season with salt and pepper.
- Serve hot, garnished with a drizzle of olive oil or fresh herbs if desired.

Ingredients

- One medium pumpkin, peeled and cubed
- Three large carrots, sliced
- One onion, chopped
- Two cloves of garlic, minced
- 4 cups vegetable broth
- 1 tsp ginger, grated
- 1/2 tsp turmeric
- Salt and pepper, to taste
- Olive oil

Nutritional Facts: (Per serving)

- Calories: 120
- Protein: 3g
- Carbohydrates: 25g
- Dietary Fiber: 6g
- Sugars: 12g
- Fat: 2g
- Sodium: 480mg

As you relish each spoonful of this Pumpkin and Carrot Soup, embrace the healing properties and the comforting warmth it brings. Ideal for chilly evenings or when you need a gentle, nourishing meal, this soup is a testament to the power of simple, wholesome ingredients working together to create something extraordinary.

Recipe 53: Chicken Vegetable Soup

Servings For: (04)

Prepping Time: 20 minutes

Cooking Time: 40 minutes

Difficulty: Easy

Experience the warmth and nourishment of this Chicken Vegetable Soup, a delicious remedy from our Anti-Inflammatory Soup Recipes collection. Packed with healthful ingredients, it's perfect for soothing and revitalizing your body.

Preparation Steps

- In a large pot, sauté the onion, garlic, carrots, and celery with a bit of oil until softened.
- Add the diced chicken and cook until no longer pink.
- Pour in the chicken broth and bring to a boil.
- Add broccoli, turmeric, and ginger. Simmer for 30 minutes.
- Season with salt and pepper.
- Serve hot and enjoy the comforting flavors.

Ingredients

- Two chicken breasts, diced
- One onion, chopped
- Two carrots, sliced
- Two celery stalks, sliced
- 1 cup broccoli florets
- 4 cups chicken broth
- Two garlic cloves, minced
- One teaspoon turmeric
- One teaspoon ginger
- Salt and pepper to taste

Nutritional Facts: (Per serving)

- Calories: 220
- Protein: 18g
- Carbohydrates: 15g
- Fat: 9g
- Sodium: 570mg
- Fiber: 3g

Conclude your day with this heartwarming Chicken Vegetable Soup, a staple in our Anti-Inflammatory Soup Recipes. Its blend of nutritious vegetables and spices provides a comforting, healing touch, making it an ideal choice for those seeking flavor and health benefits.

Recipe 54: Red Lentil Soup

Servings For: (04)

Prepping Time: 15 minutes

Cooking Time: 30 minutes

Difficulty: Easy

Discover the soothing flavors of Red Lentil Soup, an anti-inflammatory delight that's as nutritious as delicious. This recipe is a beautiful addition to any health-conscious diet, offering a comforting blend of spices and lentils.

Preparation Steps

- Rinse the lentils and set aside.
- In a large pot, sauté onion and garlic until translucent.
- Add carrots, turmeric, and cumin; cook for 2 minutes.
- Add lentils and vegetable broth; bring to a boil.
- Reduce heat, cover, and simmer for 25 minutes.
- Season with salt and pepper.
- Blend soup until smooth, if desired.
- Garnish with fresh cilantro before serving.

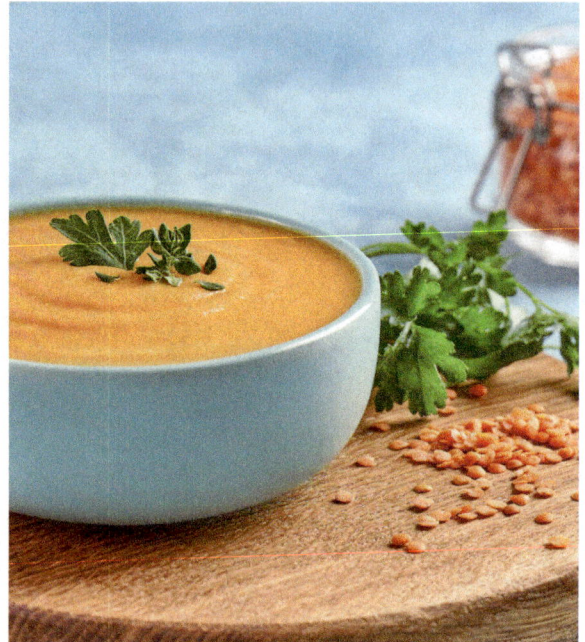

Ingredients

- 1 cup red lentils
- One large onion, chopped
- Two cloves garlic, minced
- One carrot, diced
- One teaspoon turmeric
- One teaspoon cumin
- 4 cups vegetable broth
- Salt and pepper to taste
- Fresh cilantro for garnish

Nutritional Facts: (Per serving)

- Calories: 210
- Protein: 14g
- Fiber: 15g
- Fat: 1g
- Saturated Fat: 0g
- Sodium: 300mg

Savor the warmth of this Red Lentil Soup, a dish that not only pleases the palate but also provides a wealth of health benefits. Its anti-inflammatory properties make it a perfect choice for those looking to enjoy a hearty, wholesome meal. Enjoy this simple yet satisfying soup and embrace a healthier lifestyle.

Recipe 55: Miso Soup

Servings For: (04)

Prepping Time: 15 minutes

Cooking Time: 10 minutes

Difficulty: Easy

Experience the soothing warmth of miso soup, a traditional Japanese dish known for its anti-inflammatory properties. This comforting soup combines simple ingredients to create a nourishing and delicious meal.

Preparation Steps

- Heat water in a pot over medium heat.
- Dissolve miso paste in a small amount of warm water, then add to the bank.
- Add tofu, nori, and ginger to the bank; simmer for 10 minutes.
- Stir in green onions and cook for an additional 2 minutes.
- Serve hot

Ingredients

- 4 cups water
- Two tablespoons of miso paste
- One block of tofu cubed
- Two green onions, thinly sliced
- One sheet nori (dried seaweed), cut into strips
- One teaspoon of grated ginger

Nutritional Facts: (Per serving)

- Calories: 80
- Protein: 6g
- Carbohydrates: 7g
- Dietary Fiber: 1g
- Sodium: 540mg

Enjoy the harmony of flavors in this miso soup recipe, a testament to the art of simple, healthful cooking. This soup is not just a meal; it's a gentle embrace for your body, offering the benefits of anti-inflammatory ingredients in every spoonful.

Recipe 56: Pumpkin and Apple Soup

Servings For: (04)

Prepping Time: 20 minutes

Cooking Time: 45 minutes

Difficulty: Easy

Discover the comforting blend of flavors in this Pumpkin and Apple Soup, a perfect addition to your anti-inflammatory recipe collection. This soup combines pumpkin's earthy sweetness with apples' tartness, creating a delightful balance.

Preparation Steps

- Heat the olive oil in a large pot over medium heat. Add the onions and cook until soft.
- Add the pumpkin and apples to the pot and cook for 5 minutes.
- Pour in the vegetable broth and bring to a boil.
- Reduce heat and add cinnamon, nutmeg, salt, and pepper.
- Simmer for 30 minutes or until pumpkin is tender.
- Blend the soup until smooth; adjust seasoning if needed.
- Serve warm.

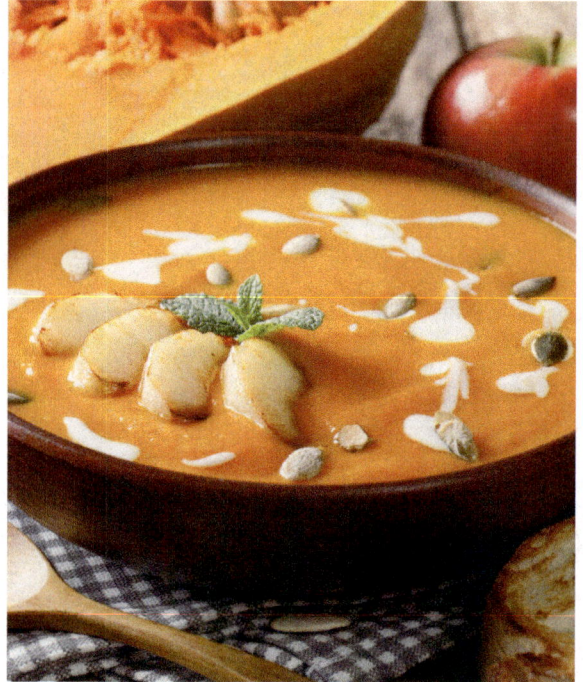

Ingredients

- One medium pumpkin, peeled and cubed
- Two apples, peeled and chopped
- One onion, chopped
- 3 cups vegetable broth
- 1 tsp ground cinnamon
- ½ tsp ground nutmeg
- Salt and pepper to taste
- 1 tbsp olive oil

Nutritional Facts: (Per serving)

- Calories: 150
- Protein: 3g
- Carbohydrates: 35g
- Fiber: 6g
- Fat: 3g
- Sodium: 700mg

Enjoy this Pumpkin and Apple Soup as a soothing, anti-inflammatory meal. Its warmth and nourishing ingredients provide a delightful culinary experience for cozy evenings. Rich in flavors and health benefits, this soup is a testament to the power of simple, natural ingredients to create something truly satisfying.

Recipe 57: Chinese Sweet Potato Soup

Servings For: (04)

Prepping Time: 20 minutes

Cooking Time: 45 minutes

Difficulty: Easy

Experience the warmth and nourishment of Chinese sweet potato soup, a delightful blend of flavors and health benefits. This anti-inflammatory recipe is perfect for soothing your body and taste buds.

Preparation Steps

- Sauté onion and garlic in a large pot until translucent.
- Add ginger and turmeric, cooking for another minute.
- Add sweet potatoes and vegetable broth; bring to a boil.
- Reduce heat and simmer until sweet potatoes are tender.
- Puree soup in batches until smooth.
- Return to pot, season with salt and pepper.
- Serve hot, garnished with cilantro.

Ingredients

- Two large sweet potatoes, peeled and cubed
- One tablespoon of ginger, minced
- 4 cups vegetable broth
- One onion, chopped
- Two cloves garlic, minced
- One teaspoon turmeric
- Salt and pepper to taste
- Fresh cilantro for garnish

Nutritional Facts: (Per serving)

- Calories: 180
- Protein: 3g
- Carbohydrates: 40g
- Fiber: 6g
- Sugar: 9g
- Fat: 1g

Enjoy this comforting Chinese sweet potato soup, a simple yet flavorful recipe that brings health and happiness to your table. It's ideal for those seeking anti-inflammatory benefits in a delicious, heartwarming meal.

Recipe 58: Cucumber Gazpacho Soup

Servings For: (04)

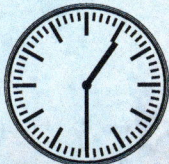

Prepping Time: 15 minutes

Cooking Time: 0 minutes

Difficulty: Easy

Discover the refreshing and healthful world of Cucumber Gazpacho Soup, an exquisite addition to your anti-inflammatory recipe collection. This chilled soup, offering a blend of crisp cucumbers, herbs, and spices, is perfect for soothing your body and tantalizing your taste buds.

Preparation Steps

- Combine cucumbers, red onion, garlic, and green bell pepper in a blender.
- Blend until smooth.
- Add olive oil, red wine vinegar, and fresh parsley.
- Season with salt and pepper.
- Blend again until all ingredients are well combined.
- Gradually add cold water to reach the desired consistency.
- Chill in the refrigerator for at least 1 hour before serving.

Ingredients

- Two large cucumbers peeled and chopped
- One small red onion, chopped
- Two cloves garlic, minced
- One green bell pepper, chopped
- Two tablespoons of olive oil
- Two tablespoons of red wine vinegar
- 1/4 cup fresh parsley, chopped
- Salt and pepper to taste
- 1 cup cold water

Nutritional Facts: (Per serving)

- Calories: 98
- Protein: 2g
- Carbohydrates: 12g
- Fat: 5g
- Fiber: 2g
- Sodium: 13mg

Conclude your meal with this Cucumber Gazpacho Soup, a delightful and nutritious dish that's as good for your health as it is for your palate. This simple, no-cook recipe offers a cooling reprieve on warm days, making it an ideal choice for a light lunch or a starter for your dinner.

Recipe 59: Beetroot Soup

Servings For: (04)

Prepping Time: 15 minutes

Cooking Time: 30 minutes

Difficulty: Easy

Indulge in the comforting warmth of Beetroot Soup, a perfect blend of taste and health. This anti-inflammatory recipe soothes your palate and benefits your body, making it an ideal choice for health-conscious individuals or those seeking culinary adventure.

Preparation Steps

- Heat the olive oil in a large pot over medium heat. Add the onions and garlic, sautéing until soft.
- Add the chopped beetroots to the pot and cook for another 5 minutes.
- Pour in the vegetable broth and bring the mixture to a boil. Reduce heat, cover, and simmer for about 20 minutes or until the beetroots are tender.
- Puree the soup using a hand blender or in batches in a regular blender.
- Stir in the lemon juice, and add salt and pepper to taste.
- Serve hot, garnished with a dollop of sour cream or yogurt and a sprinkle of fresh dill or parsley.

Ingredients

- Two medium-sized beetroots peeled and chopped
- One large onion, finely chopped
- Two cloves of garlic, minced
- 4 cups vegetable broth
- One tablespoon of olive oil
- Salt and pepper, to taste
- One teaspoon of fresh lemon juice
- Sour cream or yogurt, for garnish (optional)
- Fresh dill or parsley, for garnish (optional)

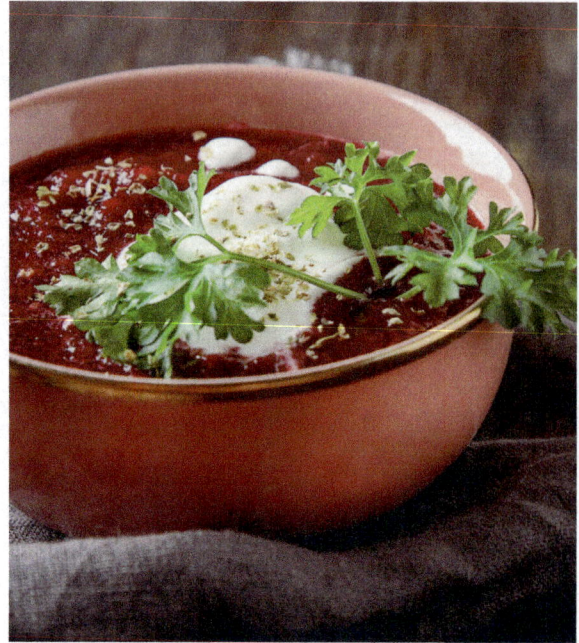

Nutritional Facts: (Per serving)

- Calories: 120
- Protein: 3g
- Carbohydrates: 18g
- Dietary Fiber: 4g
- Sugars: 12g
- Fat: 4g
- Saturated Fat: 1g
- Cholesterol: 0mg
- Sodium: 470mg

Experience the delightful fusion of flavor and health with this Beetroot Soup. It offers a vibrant and tasty meal option, and its anti-inflammatory properties also contribute to your overall well-being. This soup will become a favorite in your recipe collection, perfect for a cozy dinner or a nutritious lunch.

Recipe 60: Broccoli Cream Soup

Servings For: (04)

Prepping Time: 15 minutes

Cooking Time: 30 minutes

Difficulty: Easy

This creamy broccoli soup is a delicious and nutritious addition to any meal, especially for those seeking anti-inflammatory benefits. Packed with the goodness of broccoli, it's a comforting and healthful choice.

Preparation Steps

- Heat olive oil in a large pot over medium heat. Add onions and garlic, and sauté until softened.
- Add broccoli and vegetable broth, and bring to a boil. Reduce heat and simmer until broccoli is tender, about 20 minutes.
- Puree the soup using an immersion blender or in batches in a blender until smooth.
- Stir in heavy cream and season with salt and pepper. Heat through.

Ingredients

- 1 tbsp olive oil
- One medium onion, chopped
- Two cloves garlic, minced
- 4 cups broccoli florets
- 3 cups vegetable broth
- 1/2 cup heavy cream
- Salt and pepper, to taste

Nutritional Facts: (Per serving)

- Calories: 200
- Protein: 5g
- Carbohydrates: 15g
- Fat: 14g
- Dietary Fiber: 4g
- Sodium: 300mg

This broccoli cream soup, rich in anti-inflammatory properties, is a perfect blend of health and taste. It's an ideal choice for a cozy dinner or as a starter, offering both comfort and nourishment.

Conclusions

Embark on a journey to wellness and delight with Shirley Macy's "Easy Anti-Inflammatory Recipes Cookbook," where health and flavor unite in a symphony of culinary excellence. This isn't just another cookbook; it's your companion in a quest for a healthier, more vibrant life.

Within these pages, you'll discover 60 carefully curated recipes, each an adventure for your taste buds. A renowned nutrition expert, Shirley Macy, has meticulously designed these dishes to combat inflammation, the silent culprit behind many chronic health issues. Imagine savoring meals that not only tantalize your palate but also contribute to your well-being. From zesty breakfasts to nourishing dinners, each recipe is a testament to Shirley's commitment to delicious, healthy eating.

Picture yourself flipping through the high-quality photographs accompanying each recipe, visual feasts that promise the joy of cooking and the pleasure of eating. The Kindle and Paperback versions ensure that whether you're a digital enthusiast or a lover of traditional cookbooks, your journey to a healthier lifestyle is always at your fingertips. Easy instructions and accessible ingredients make these anti-inflammatory meals a breeze, turning even novice cooks into culinary artists.

It's your turn to transform your kitchen into a health haven. Whether you're battling inflammation, seeking healthier meal options, or love to explore new recipes, "Easy Anti-Inflammatory Recipes Cookbook" is your key to a treasure trove of delightful, wholesome meals. Don't just take our word for it; experience it yourself. Embrace this opportunity to nourish your body, entice your senses, and enrich your life. Grab your copy today in Kindle or Paperbag format, and let Shirley Macy guide you on this exciting culinary journey.

Printed in Great Britain
by Amazon

41428195R00073